LAST TESTAMENT

LAST TESTAMENT

In his own words

Pope Benedict XVI
With Peter Seewald

translated by Jacob Phillips

BLOOMSBURY

LONDON · OXFORD · NEW YORK · NEW DELHI · SYDNEY

Bloomsbury Continuum
An imprint of Bloomsbury Publishing Plc

50 Bedford Square
London
WC1B 3DP
UK

1385 Broadway
New York
NY 10018
USA

www.bloomsbury.com

Bloomsbury, Continuum and the Diana logo are trademarks of Bloomsbury Publishing Plc

First published 2016.

Originally published in German as *Benedikt XVI: Letzte Gespräche mit Peter Seewald* © 2016 Droemer Verlag. An imprint of Verlagsgruppe Droemer Knaur GMbH & Co. KG.

British Library Cataloguing-in-Publication Data
A catalogue record for this book is available from the British Library.

Library of Congress Cataloguing-in-Publication data has been applied for.

ISBN:	HB:	978-1-4729-4467-2
	EXPORT TPB:	978-1-4729-4461-0
	EPDF:	978-1-4729-4460-3
	EPUB:	978-1-4729-4463-4

2 4 6 8 10 9 7 5 3

Typeset by Integra Software Services Pvt. Ltd.
Printed and bound in the U.S.A. by Berryville Graphics Inc., Berryville, Virginia

To find out more about our authors and books visit www.bloomsbury.com. Here you will find extracts, author interviews, details of forthcoming events and the option to sign up for our newsletters.

'Faith is nothing other than the touch of God's hand in the night of the world, and so — in the silence — to hear the word, to see love.'

Benedict XVI at the close of the Lenten retreat for the Roman Curia, before the end of his pontificate, 23 February 2013

Contents

Foreword

One Last Visit

A summer and a winter had passed, and as I once again made my way up the steep path to the Mater Ecclesiae convent in the Vatican Gardens on 23 May 2016, I was fearful that this could be our last full-length conversation.

Sister Carmela opened the door. She was not wearing an apron this time, but was dressed in elegant clothes. Hanging in the reception room was a picture of St Augustine, that great spiritual teacher who meant so much to Benedict XVI, because he too is driven by that dramatic human struggle to scrutinize the truth of the faith.

Instead of red slippers, he now wore sandals like a monk. He has been blind in his left eye for many years, he remembers less and less now, and meanwhile his hearing has diminished. His body had grown very thin, but his whole demeanour was tender like never before. And it was fascinating to see that this bold thinker, the philosopher of God, the first person to call himself *Pope Emeritus*, has arrived at last at a place where the intellect alone is not enough: a place of silence and prayer, the pulsing heart of faith.

It was November 1992 when I first encountered the then Prefect of the Faith. The editors of the magazine supplement to the *Süddeutsche Zeitung* wanted to publish an article about him, and I was to write it. On a list of applicants scrapping for an appointment with the most famous cardinal in the world were the names of journalists from the *New York Times*, *Pravda* and *Le Figaro*. I was hardly one to be considered particularly Catholic, but the more time I spent with Joseph Ratzinger, the more his sovereignty impressed me, as did his passion, and his courage to go against the grain with his old-fashioned thinking. And strangely, these findings were not only shocking, they also seemed to be right.

The much-maligned '*Panzerkardinal*', understood properly, embodied not so much a relic from the past, as something for the future: a new intelligence for recognizing and articulating the mysteries of the faith. His speciality was the ability to unravel complicated issues, to see straight through mere superficialities. Science and religion, physics and metaphysics, thought and prayer – Ratzinger brought these things together again in order to arrive at the genuine core of an issue. In the beauty of his language, the depth of his thinking leads one up to the heights. 'Theology', he explained, 'is pondering what God has said and thought before us.'[1] In order to be able to receive this freely, one must also be listening. If one is not only to impress people, but rather lead them to God, one needs the inspired Word.

Like Karol Wojtyla, Joseph Ratzinger had first-hand experience of the consequences of an atheist system. As a child he watched as crucifixes disappeared from schools, and when he was a seventeen-year-old soldier,

---

[1] *The Nature and Mission of Theology: Essays to Orient Theology in Today's Debates*, San Francisco: Ignatius Press, 1995, p. 104. [Footnotes compiled by Jacob Phillips]

he saw the insanity of a world without God creating a 'new man', which ended in terror and apocalyptic devastation. The task of having to use reasoned argument to defend Christianity against the transvaluation of values would mark his thinking, his whole oeuvre. 'In the faith of my parents', he said, 'I found the confirmation that Catholicism had been a bulwark of truth and justice against that regime of atheism and lies represented by National Socialism.'[2]

His life ran a dramatic course strewn with triumphs and failures, during which this highly gifted man understood himself to be one of those called to ascend to the chair of Peter.

There is the sensitive schoolboy who composes Greek hexameters and loves Mozart. The very young student who dreams of a Christian awakening among the bombed-out streets of Munich. The inquisitive model student, trained in the progressive thinking of the best theologians of the age, who broods for hours over books by Augustine, Kierkegaard and Newman. The unconventional curate who enthuses groups of young people. But also the devastated post-doctoral candidate, whose young career stands on the brink, threatened with collapse.

Destiny decreed things differently. In the blink of an eye the almost boyish-seeming professor from a tiny village in Bavaria becomes a rising star in the theological firmament.

People sit up and take notice: of the fresh-sounding phrases, the creative ways to enter into the gospel, and the authentic doctrine which he embodies. 'In the

---

[2] Joseph Ratzinger, *The Ratzinger Report*, San Francisco: Ignatius Press, 1985, p. 166.

theology of a great thinker', wrote his mentor from Munich, Gottlieb Söhngen, 'the substance and the form of theological thinking reciprocally interplay to shape a living unity.' Ratzinger's lecture halls are full to bursting. Written notes from his lectures are passed around, and copied out thousands of times by hand. His *Introduction to Christianity* excites Karol Wojtyla in the Académie des Sciences Morales et Politiques in Paris, an academy of the Institut de France which he will later join himself.

Ratzinger is just thirty-five years old when he is deeply stirred by the openness of the Second Vatican Council, which seeks to bring the Church into the modern world. No one besides this theological adolescent, a grateful John XXIII pointed out, was able to improve on the way Ratzinger expressed what the initiator of the Council actually intended.

While the theologians celebrated as progressives accommodated themselves to rather petit-bourgeois conceptions, and largely just served the mainstream, Ratzinger remained restless: as professor, as Bishop of Munich, and as Prefect for the Congregation of the Faith in Rome, where he kept John Paul II's back covered for a quarter of a century and administered plenty of lashings. 'The real problem at this moment of our history', he warned, 'is that God is disappearing from the human horizon.' By 'extinguishing the light of God's approach', humanity is losing its bearings, 'with increasingly evident destructive effects'.[3]

[3] From the *Letter of His Holiness Pope Benedict XVI to the Bishops of the Catholic Church Concerning the Remission of the Excommunication of the Four Bishops Consecrated by Archbishop Lefebvre*, 10 March 2009.

He did not exempt his Church from criticism. Already by 1958 he was speaking of the need for a 'detachment from the world'.[4] This is necessary, he claimed, so that the active potency of the faith can be revealed again. We have to remain steadfast and unaccommodating, in order to demonstrate, without any frivolity, that Christianity is intertwined with a worldview that reaches beyond everything linked with a secular, materialistic attitude. The Christian worldview involves the revelation of the eternal God. It is naïve to think you need only dress all in different clothes, speak as the world speaks, and then suddenly all will be well. We must find our way back to an authentic proclamation, and a liturgy that brings the radiant mystery of the mass to light.

The indictment he gave in contemplating the *Via Crucis* on Good Friday 2005 was unforgettable. 'How much filth there is in the Church,' he cried out, 'and even among those who, being in the priesthood, ought to belong entirely to him.'[5]

The aged cardinal had become a sort of yardstick against which no one wanted to be assessed. But a few days after this call for self-examination and purification, he walked through the curtains of the loggia of St Peter's Basilica as the 264th successor of the first apostle, before a jubilant throng of humanity. He was the 'little Pope', a simple worker in the vineyard of the Lord, following the towering Karol Wojtyla. He introduced himself to the 1.2 billion Catholics across the globe – and he knew what needed to be done.

[4] Joseph Ratzinger, 'Die neuen Heiden und die Kirche', *Hochland* 51 (1958/9) pp. 1–11.
[5] From the meditation on the 9th Station of the Cross, given by Cardinal Joseph Ratzinger at the Colosseum, 25 March 2005.

The new Pope made it clear that the true problems of the Church lie not in a dwindling membership, but in a dwindling faith. The extinguishing of a Christian consciousness is causing the crisis, the lukewarmness in prayer and worship, the neglect of mission. For him, true reform is a question of inner awakening, of setting hearts on fire. The top priority is to proclaim what we can know and believe with certainty about Christ.

For many years the German pontificate was met with a single hosanna. Never before had so many people attended papal audiences. Benedict's encyclicals, *Deus caritus est*, *Spe salvi*, and *Caritas in veritate*, reached astronomically high numbers of reprints. Many of his books had long since become classics, and now his speeches provided headlines for the front pages of the world's press. Managing to undertake the transition from the long and profound papacy of John Paul II single-handedly, and without rupture, was a unique achievement.

But the seventy-eight-year-old was not only the Pope who helped shape the Council; he also dreamed of the Council. His style was characterized by level-headedness, dialogue, and a focus on the essentials. Liturgical extravagance was reduced, synods of bishops cut short, and discussions structured collegially instead.

Benedict XVI worked quietly, even on things left behind by his predecessor. He rejected showmanship. He quietly abolished the tradition of kissing the Pope's hand, he replaced the powerful papal crown on his coat of arms with a simple bishop's mitre. But out of respect for tradition he also adopted conventions which were not necessarily to his taste. He was not the boss, not an icon of the Church, he urged. He only stood in the place of another, who alone must be believed in and loved: Jesus Christ, the Word of God made man.

After John Paul II, Benedict XVI was the second successor of Peter to speak in a mosque. But this German pontiff was the first Pope to participate in a Protestant service. For the leader of the Catholic Church to visit Luther's study was an historic act of unparalleled scale. He also set precedents by installing a Protestant as chairman of the Pontifical Academy of Sciences, and bringing a Muslim professor to the Pontifical University. At the same time, he raised the papacy to a new dimension through his theological and intellectual potency, which made the Catholic Church attractive even to outsiders. This happened not least through the rich content of his three themed years, the Year of Paul, the Year of Priests, and the Year of Faith. With the Apostolic Letter *Summorum Pontificum* he allowed priests to celebrate the Tridentine form of the mass again, a form which was valid for centuries, but not without first having to request approval from the bishops. It was not a retrograde move, but an act of openness and freedom.

Benedict XVI did not do everything right. Without doubt his papacy did not completely realize its full potential. Many times, the behaviour of his brothers in the episcopacy amounted to non-compliance, as did that of some in the Vatican's governmental apparatus. Relentless criticism generated the countless cover stories and articles in the media that assailed Ratzinger. The besieged pontiff responded by saying that 'If a Pope is only getting applause, he has to ask himself whether or not he is doing things right.' To name a few of these punishing 'scandals': with Richard

Williamson, a bishop of the Society of St Pius X, the Pope had 'admitted a Holocaust denier back into the Catholic Church', or so runs the indictment still maintained to this day. This reportage actually brought a turning point in general attitudes to the Pope's work, which had hitherto been extremely positive for wide sections of the public. The truth of the matter, however, is that Williamson was an Anglican convert. He was neither accepted as a bishop by Rome, nor rehabilitated by the Society of St Pius X, which was separated from the Catholic Church.

The topic of Jewish–Christian relations remained among Ratzinger's primary concerns. The secretary general of the World Jewish Congress from 2001 to 2007, Israel Singer, said that without him, the decisive and historic change in attitude of the Catholic Church in relation to Judaism would not have been possible. Singer says this change put a definite end to the attitude in the Church that had prevailed for a thousand years. Maram Stern, vice-president of the World Congress, summarizes the matter by saying that this relationship is now better 'than at any prior moment in history'.

As regards the scandal surrounding sexual abuse committed by those entrusted with care as priests and religious, there have in fact been many failings and errors, especially by the various authorities in individual countries. But it has also long since been acknowledged that without Benedict XVI's management, one of the greatest crises in the history of the Catholic Church would have caused even more damage. As Prefect of the Congregation of the Faith, Ratzinger had already initiated steps to resolve cases systematically, and to punish the perpetrators. As Pope he dismissed some 400 priests, and defined the canonical basis on which to prosecute bishops and cardinals who failed to comply with the corrective measures.

And the Vatileaks affair? One must not trivialize it. Hidden behind the events were problematic dysfunctions in several of the world Church's corridors of power. But all that is left of the alleged 'conspiracy in the Vatican', in the end, is nothing more than the theft of papers by a valet who was psychologically unwell. Regarding the controversial Vatican bank Istituto per le Opere di Religione (Institute for the Works of Religion), Benedict had commissioned an extensive inspection, and initiated the bank's reorganization, not least in arranging for an investigation of its entire field of operation. The commission's report on this is under lock and key. Its scope, however, is far less dramatic than indicated.

Everyone misses Benedict's hallmarks: his wise speeches which could cool the mind and warm the heart, the richness of his words, the honesty of his analysis, the infinite patience in his listening, the nobility of character that he embodied like no other churchman. There is his shy smile as well, of course, and then his often rather clumsy movements as he walked across a stage – a bit like Charlie Chaplin. But above all there is his insistence on reason, which, as the guarantor of faith, protects religion from lapsing into erroneous fantasies and dangerous fanaticism. Not to mention his modernity, which many were either unable or unwilling to acknowledge. He has remained faithful, even in the willingness to do things which no one had done before.

Notwithstanding the abundance of his writings, sermons, meditations, letters – there are 30,000 letters just from the time before his appointment as bishop – Joseph Ratzinger never developed his own theological system. As a theologian he took on what was there, discerned its essentials, situated it in relation to the context of the time, and then expressed it anew – to preserve the message of the gospel and the accrued knowledge of the Christian past for generations to come. Given the significance which he thereby assigned to the Church, his struggle for this Church is understandable – he wanted it to remain the barque of salvation in space and time, a Noah's Ark for the transmission of a better world. He called this, 'the eschatological radicalism of the Christian revolution'.[6]

The three-volume work on Jesus Christ, on its own, makes this pontificate unique. With it, Benedict XVI created a handbook for the future of theology, catechesis and priestly formation – in short, a foundation for the teaching of the faith for the third millennium. It was not on a professorial chair, but on the chair of Peter, that things could come full circle. And there was no one else with the educational formation, the background, the strength and the inspiration, to make the image of Jesus transparent again, with intellectual meticulousness and a level-headed spirituality, after it had been obscured beyond recognition. Thus humanity could now approach this image afresh.

The English historian Peter Watson called Benedict XVI one of the 'last representatives of the German

---

[6] See Joseph Ratzinger, *Eschatology: Death and Eternal Life*, Washington DC: Catholic University of America Press, 1988 [1977], p. 49.

genius', putting him on a par with Lessing, Kant and Beethoven.[7] For the Peruvian winner of the Nobel Prize for Literature, Mario Vargas Llosa, he is one of the most significant intellectuals of the present, whose 'new and bold reflections' provide answers to the moral, cultural and existential problems of our time.[8] History will judge what significance this Pope deserves, from a vantage point beyond today's horizon. However, one thing can already be considered certain: no one besides Joseph Ratzinger has stood for so long – over three decades – by the helm of the biggest and oldest institution in the world. With his contributions to the Council, the rediscovery of the Fathers, the bringing to life of doctrine, and the purification and consolidation of the Church, he was not only a renewer of the faith, but also, as a theologian on the chair of Peter, one of the most significant popes ever, the modern world's Doctor of the Church, of a sort that will not be seen again. The historic act of his resignation has fundamentally changed the office of Peter at the last. He gave it back the spiritual dimension to which it was assigned at the beginning.

With Benedict XVI, an era comes to an end, perhaps even an aeon – one of those chapters of history which in the passing of millennia denote the major turning points of history. The eight years of his papacy were something like the great retreat the Church needed, to buttress the interior castle and to strengthen her soul. Seen in this way, the last Pope of a declining epoch has built the bridge for the coming of the new – no matter

[7] See Peter Watson, *The German Genius: Europe's Third Renaissance, the Second Scientific Revolution, and the Twentieth Century*, London: Simon & Schuster 2010, pp. 786–8.
[8] See http://elpais.com/elpais/2013/02/21/opinion/1361447726_090824.html.

how that new epoch will look. By the verdict of his followers, Benedict XVI was 'a great Pope': 'great due to the vitality and penetrating power of his intelligence, great due to his major contributions to theology, great due to his love for the Church and for humanity, and great due to his virtue and his religiosity'. In the words of Pope Francis, his spirit 'will manifest itself more greatly and more forcefully, from generation to generation'.[9]

The following interviews were conducted shortly before and after Benedict's resignation, as background discussion for working on his biography. They provide a further glimpse of one of the most fascinating personalities of our time. The text was read by the Pope Emeritus and approved for this edition. May this book be a small contribution towards correcting false images and shining light into darkness, particularly on the circumstances surrounding the act of resignation which left the world breathless. It is, in the end, written in order to better understand the human being Joseph Ratzinger and the shepherd Benedict XVI, to appreciate his holiness, and above all to keep open the doors to his work, for therein lies a store of treasure for future years.

Peter Seewald

[9] See http://kath.net/news/48069.

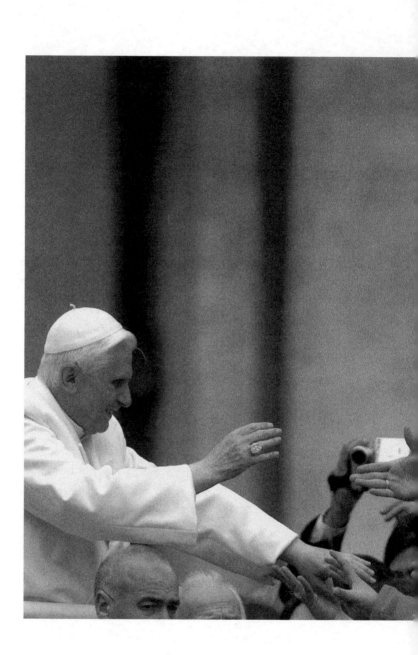

PART ONE

The Bells of Rome

I

Quiet Days in Mater Ecclesiae

Pope Benedict, as the Holy Father you were acclaimed by millions, you lived in a palace, and you welcomed dignitaries from across the world. Do you miss it at all?

Not at all, no! On the contrary, I am grateful to God for lifting this responsibility which I could no longer bear from my shoulders. I am grateful that I am now free humbly to walk with Him, to live among, and be visited by, friends.

Suddenly to be completely without power, virtually locked away in the walls of the Vatican – how does that feel?

I never accepted 'power' so that I would be in any way strong, but always as a responsibility, as something difficult and burdensome, something which causes one to ask oneself every day: have I done right? Even with the acclamation of the people, I always knew the people weren't directing this at this lowly little man here, but at the one I represented. So it is not difficult to relinquish the office.

Early on you predicted that your pontificate could be short, due to your age and the state of your health.

I did think that I might not have that much strength, yes.

Eight years was longer than many of your predecessors. First off, did your attitude not have consequences for the programme you set for your time in office?

Clearly. I could not start any long-term things. One has to make do with what time one has. I was conscious that my task was of another kind: that I must try above all else to show what faith means in the contemporary world, and further, to highlight the centrality of faith in God, and give people the courage to have faith, courage to live concretely in the world with faith. Faith, reason, these were all things I recognized as central to my mission, and for these things it was not important to have a long pontificate.

Was there a moment in which you prayed to God and said: 'Release me, I can't go on, I don't want to go on?'

Not in that way, no. I mean, I did pray to the loving God − especially when one thinks of the Williamson situation − to get me out of this situation and to help me, certainly. But I knew He had put me in this place, and so He would not let me fall.

You never once thought you would drop the whole load? Never once that you need not always be in service, with endless obligations, with all those banalities of office that threaten to overwhelm someone? Just to be a human being for once?

Yes, there were of course times like that, naturally. I often said that to the Pope, especially as Cardinal Prefect.[1] But John Paul II always said: 'No, there's more to do!'

---

[1] Joseph Ratzinger was Cardinal Prefect of the Congregation for the Doctrine of the Faith (CDF) from 1981 to 2005.

Did you not, then, ask yourself whether you should not accept the result of the conclave at all?

It was in fact a very serious question for me. However, what impressed me was that even before the conclave many cardinals have exhorted the one who would be elected, so to speak, saying he must – even if he doesn't feel up to taking the cross upon himself – submit himself to the two-thirds majority, and see that decision as a sign. This is his inner duty. It is worked out with so much gravity and dignity that I believed, if the majority of the cardinals really elect me, the Lord is electing me, and then I must accept it.

So there was never a point at which you said to yourself: 'Maybe I was the wrong choice?'

No. The cardinals had voted, so the one chosen must undertake his task. And it isn't the judgement of journalists that matters, but the judgement of the loving God.

You yearned greatly to be able to live only in contemplation and prayer. Can you do that now?

Not entirely. First, it is not possible due to my psychological strength, because I am simply not inwardly strong enough to dedicate myself constantly to divine and spiritual things, but there are also outside pressures, because visitors come. I do think it is good that I have dialogues with people who carry responsibility for the Church today or who play a role in my life, and who help me to remain anchored in human things, so to speak.

Will you still write?

No! No, no, I knew after Christmas: this is *Nunc dimittis*; I have done my work.[i]

Are there diaries or notebooks?

No diaries, but I have written down some reflections at certain intervals, which I am disposing of.

Why?

[Laughs] Because it is too personal.

But that would be—

A field day for the historians.

You have produced a great theological oeuvre like no Pope before you, your books selling millions. Don't you find it terribly difficult not to pick up your pen?

Not at all, no. I mean, I still write my Sunday sermon every week. In this sense I have the intellectual task of interpreting the Scriptures. But I could not write any more. There needs to be methodical work behind writing, and that would simply be too arduous for me now.

You write sermons for four or five people?

Why not? [Laughs] Certainly! Whether there are three or twenty or a thousand. The Word of God must always be present to people.

Are there things which you would still want to make sure you achieve?

Not in the sense that I still have something I want to leave for humanity. But certainly in the sense of continuing in my service of prayer.

Bequests?

After having written a will previously at various points in my life, my final will is now well fixed.

A theological testament?

No, no. [Laughs] No, I only have objects and I'm leaving them behind.

What do the meditations of a Papa emeritus look like? Are certain intellectual tasks particularly dear and valuable to you today?

Well, I can now pray the breviary deeply and slowly and thereby deepen my friendship with the Psalms, with the Fathers. And every Sunday, as I mentioned, I compose a little homily. I let my thoughts be orientated towards that over the whole course of the week, so they mature slowly, so I can sound out a text from many different angles. What is it saying to me? What is it saying to the people here in the monastery? That is what is actually new, if I may put it so: tuning in to the prayer of the Psalms with even more silence, making myself more familiar with it. And in this way the texts of the liturgy, above all the Sunday readings, accompany me throughout the week.

Do you have a favourite prayer?

Indeed, there are some. There is this from St Ignatius: 'Take Lord, all my liberty . . .' Then from Francis

Xavier: 'I do not love you because you can give me paradise or condemn me to hell, but because you are my God.' Or from Nicholas of Flüe: 'Take me, as I am . . .' And then the one I like most – what I would have liked to have seen included in *Gotteslob*[2] but forgot to propose – the 'general prayer' by Peter Canisius from the sixteenth century. It remains unchangingly pertinent and beautiful.[ii]

Your favourite spiritual place?

I would say Altötting,[3] naturally.

The central point of your reflections was always the personal encounter with Christ. How is that now? How close have you come to Jesus?

[Deep intake of breath] Well, naturally that is relative to different situations, but in the liturgy, in prayer, in contemplations for Sunday's sermon, I see him directly before me. He is of course always great and full of mystery. I now find many statements from the Gospels more challenging in their greatness and gravity than I did before. Indeed, this recalls an episode from my time as a chaplain. One day Romano Guardini was a guest of the neighbouring Protestant parish, and said to the Protestant pastor, 'in old age it doesn't get easier, but harder'. That deeply impacted on and moved my then

---

[2] *Gotteslob* is an authorized hymnbook of the Catholic dioceses of Germany. Today's edition was revised in 2013, but the Pope Emeritus is probably referring to the possibility of having proposed this hymn for the original 1975 edition.

[3] Altötting is a Bavarian town next to Benedict XVI's birthplace of Marktl am Inn, a pilgrimage destination with a revered statue of the Virgin Mary where he worshipped as a child and which he visited while Pope in 2006.

priest. But there is something true in it. On the one hand, in old age you are more deeply practised, so to speak. Life has taken its shape. The fundamental decisions have been made. On the other hand, one feels the difficulty of life's questions more deeply, one feels the weight of today's godlessness, the weight of the absence of faith which goes deep into the Church, but then one also feels the greatness of Jesus Christ's words, which evade interpretation more often than before.

Is this connected to a loss of God's nearness? Or with doubt?

Not doubt, but one feels how far one is removed from the greatness of the mystery. Of course new insights are opened up again and again. I find this touching and comforting. But one also notices that the depths of the Word are never fully plumbed. And some words of wrath, of rejection, of the threat of judgement, certainly become more mysterious and grave and awesome than before.

One imagines that the Pope, the representative of Christ on earth, must have a particularly close, intimate relationship to the Lord.

Yes, it should be that way, and I did not have the feeling that he was far away. I am always able to speak with him inwardly. But I am nevertheless just a lowly little man who does not always reach all the way up to him.

Do you experience the 'dark nights' of which the saints speak?

Not as intensely. Maybe because I am not holy enough to get so deep into the darkness. But when things just happen in the sphere of human events, where one says: 'How can the loving God permit that?', the questions are certainly very big questions. Then one must maintain firmly, in faith, that He knows better.

Have these 'dark nights' existed in your life at all?

Let's say they've not darkened the whole, but the difficulty so often with God is the question of why there's so much evil and so forth; how something can be reconciled with His almighty power, with His goodness, and this certainly assails faith in different situations time and again.

How does one deal with such problems of faith?

Primarily by the fact that I do not let go of the foundational certainty of faith, because I stand in it, so to speak,[4] but also because I know if I do not understand something that doesn't mean that it is wrong, but that I am too small for it. With many things it has been like this: I gradually grew to see it this way. More and more it is a gift; you suddenly see something which was not perceptible before. You realize that you must be humble, you must wait when you can't enter into a passage of the Scriptures, until the Lord opens it up for you.

And does He open it up?

Not always. But the fact that such moments of realization happen signifies something great for me in itself.

Does a Papa emeritus *fear death? Or fear dying at least?*

---

[4] This calls to mind one of the most celebrated passages of Joseph Ratzinger's writing, where he describes faith as 'standing firm', in *Introduction to Christianity*, London: Burns & Oates, 1969, pp. 39ff.

In a certain respect, yes. For one thing there is the fear that one is imposing on people through a long period of disability. I would find that very distressing. My father always had a fear of death too; it has endured with me, but lessened. Another thing is that, despite all the confidence I have that the loving God cannot forsake me, the closer you come to his face, the more intensely you feel how much you have done wrong. In this respect the burden of guilt always weighs on someone, but the basic trust is of course always there.

What bears heavily on you?

Well, that you have not done enough for people, not treated people rightly. Oh, there are so many details, not very significant things – thanks be to God – but just so many things where you have to say that something could and should have been done better.

So when you stand before the Almighty, what will you say to him?

I will plead with him to show leniency towards my wretchedness.

The believer trusts that 'eternal life' is a life fulfilled.

Definitely! Then he is truly at home.

What are you expecting?

There are various dimensions. Some are more theological. St Augustine says something which is a great thought and a great comfort here. He interprets the passage from the Psalms 'seek his face always' as saying:

this applies 'for ever'; to all eternity.[5] God is so great that we never finish our searching. He is always new. With God there is perpetual, unending encounter, with new discoveries and new joy. Such things are theological matters. At the same time, in an entirely human perspective, I look forward to being reunited with my parents, my siblings, my friends, and I imagine it will be as lovely as it was at our family home.

Eschatology, the doctrine of the 'last things' – death, purgatory, the dawn of a new world – is one of the fundamental themes of your work, what the book you consider your best is about. Are you able to profit from your theology today, when you personally stand immediately before these eschatological questions?

Indeed, especially what I considered about purgatory, about the nature of pain, the meaning it has, and also about the communal character of beatitude. I think about these because it is very important to me to believe that one is immersed in a great ocean of joy and love, so to speak.

Do you consider yourself one of the enlightened?

No I don't! [Laughs] No.

But is enlightenment, next to holiness, not also a definite goal of the Catholic life in Christ?

Now, the concept 'enlightened' has something a little elitist about it. I am an entirely average Christian. Naturally Christianity is about a concern to recognize

[5] Ps. 105.4.

the truth, which is light. By virtue of faith a simple man is enlightened, because he sees what others, who are so clever, cannot perceive. In this sense, faith is enlightenment. Baptism in Greek means a *photism*, an enlightenment, a coming into the light, becoming one who sees. My eyes are then opened. I see this dimension which is wholly other, something it is not possible for me to perceive with the eyes of the body alone.

2

The Resignation

Now we come to that decision which in itself already makes your pontificate seem historic. Your resignation was the first time a genuinely ruling pontiff had stood down from his office. No one else has changed the papacy more deeply in modern times than you, with this revolutionary act. The Petrine foundation has come closer to us; it is more modern, and in a certain sense more human. Already in 2010 you explained in your book, Light of the World, *that if a pope is physically or psychologically no longer in a position to maintain office, he has the right and in some cases even the duty to step back from his job. Was there nevertheless a fierce inner struggle with this decision?*

[Deep intake of breath] Of course it was not entirely easy. No Pope has stood down for a thousand years; it was still an exception in the first thousand years of the papacy. It is a decision which was not taken easily, and which had to be mulled over again and again. On the other hand, the evidence was so great that there was no internal struggle. An awareness of its responsibility and seriousness called for the most thorough examination, time and again having to examine yourself before God and before yourself; that took place, yes, but not in the sense that it tore me to pieces.

Had you judged that your decision was also a disappointment, something that would cause bewilderment?

That was perhaps more intense than I thought it would be, because friends, people, were stopped in their tracks at my news. For them it was serious and ground-breaking; at that moment they were really distressed and felt forsaken.

Did you take into account the shock it would cause?

I had to accept it, yes.

It must have expended an incredible amount of energy.

With matters like these one is helped. But it was also clear to me that I had to do it and that this was the right moment. People then also accepted this. Many are grateful that there is now a new Pope approaching them with a new style. Others may still mourn somewhat, but they have also come to be grateful. They know that my hour had passed and I had given all I could give.

When was your mind made up?

I would say during the summer holiday of 2012.

August?

Thereabouts, yes.

Were you in a depression?

Not a depression, no, but things weren't going well for me. I realized the trip to Mexico and Cuba had really taken it out of me. The doctor also said to me that I could not fly over the Atlantic again. As scheduled, World Youth Day was supposed to be in Rio in 2014. Because of the football World Cup it was brought forward by one year. It was clear to me that I must step down in plenty of time for the new Pope to plan for Rio. In this respect the decision matured gradually after the Mexico–Cuba trip. Otherwise I would have had to try holding out until 2014. But I knew that I could no longer manage it.

How does one manage to carry out a decision on this scale without anyone to talk with about it?

You talk about it extensively with the loving God.

Did you confide in your brother?

Not immediately, but I did. Yes, yes.

Until shortly before the announcement, only four people had been confided in. Was there a reason for this?

Yes of course, because the moment the people knew, the mandate would crumble, since its authority disintegrates then. It was also important that my position was genuinely occupied and my service could be done fully up to the last.

Were you afraid someone would talk you out of taking this step?

No [amused laughter], I mean, there was that, but I wasn't fearful because I had an inner certainty that it had to be done, and that isn't something you can be talked out of.

When and by whom was the text of your resignation speech written?

By me. I couldn't tell you now exactly when, but I wrote it at the most fourteen days beforehand.

Why in Latin?

Because you do something so important in Latin. Furthermore, Latin is the language that I've so mastered that I can write in it properly. I could have written it in Italian, but with the danger that there would be a couple of mistakes in it.

You wanted to resign originally in December, but then settled on 11 February, Rose Monday, feast day of Our Lady of Lourdes.[1] Does this have a symbolic significance?

I was not aware of the fact that it was Rose Monday. This caused disturbances in Germany. It was the day of Madonna of Lourdes. The feast of Bernadette of Lourdes is on my birthday though. In this sense there are connections, and it seems right to me that I did it on this day.

So this moment in time has . . .

. . . certainly an inner connection, yes.

How do you remember this historic day? It can be assumed you didn't sleep particularly well the night before.

But it's not all bad. To the general public, of course, it was a new and tremendous step, which is how I saw it.

[1] Rose Monday (*Rosenmontag*) is in some German-speaking regions the highlight of the Carnival before Lent; it is the Monday before Shrove Tuesday.

But I had wrestled with it inwardly the whole time, so my inward self was to some extent already weathered. In this sense it was not a day of particular suffering for me.

Did everything go as normal that morning, with the usual routine?

I would say so, yes.

The same prayers . . .?

The same prayers, and, of course, a couple said intensively for that hour, certainly.

You didn't awake earlier, or eat breakfast late?

No, no.

Around seventy cardinals sat in a horseshoe shape in the huge hall with the beautiful name Sala del Concistoro.[2] It was a consistory scheduled to announce various canonizations, so as you entered the room no one could have expected what was going to happen.

We had planned a couple of canonizations, yes.

The astonishment began as you started to speak in Latin: 'Dearly esteemed cardinals, I have not gathered you together only to let you participate in the canonizations, but I also have something of great importance to tell you.' Everyone was already confused. As you continued reciting your statement, some faces came over petrified, others in disbelief, or helpless,

---

[2] The 'Hall of the Consistory' is in the Apostolic Palace in Vatican City.

astounded. When the dean of the College of Cardinals, Angelo Sodano, first took the floor, all that had happened became clear. Did the cardinals speak to you immediately afterwards, or bombard you, even?

[Laughs] No, that would not happen. After the consistory the Pope goes out solemnly, so no one bombards him. In such situations the Pope is sovereign.

On this day, about which historians still write, what was going through your head?

The question: 'What will mankind be saying as I stand there?', of course. It was a sad day in my household, naturally. I brought myself before the Lord in a particular way throughout the day. But there was nothing specific.

In the resignation speech the reason you gave for relinquishing your office was the diminishing of your energy. But is a slow-down in the ability to perform, reason enough to climb down from the chair of Peter?

One can of course make that accusation, but it would be a functional misunderstanding. The follower of Peter is not merely bound to a function; the office enters into your very being. In this regard, fulfilling a function is not the only criterion. Then again, the Pope must do concrete things, must keep the whole situation in his sights, must know which priorities to set, and so on. This ranges from receiving heads of state, receiving bishops – with whom one must be able to enter into a deeply intimate conversation – to the decisions which come each day. Even if you say a few of these things can be struck off, there remain so many things which are essential, that, if the capability to do them is no longer there – for me anyway; someone else might see it otherwise – now's the time to free up the chair.

Cardinal Reginald Pole (1500–58), to whom you referred in a lecture, says in his theology of the cross: the cross is the authentic place of the representative of Christ. There is a martyrological structure of the papal primacy.

That was deeply moving to me then. I'd had a dissertation written about him by one of my students.[3] It is certainly enduringly true, and thus the Pope must each day bear witness, must take up his cross each day and always be a *martyr*, in the sense of being a martyr to the sufferings of the world and its problems. That is something very important. If a pope were only ever applauded, he would have to ask himself whether or not he was doing things right. The message of Christ is a scandal for the world, beginning with Christ himself. There will always be opposition, and the Pope must be a sign of contradiction. This is a criterion which concerns him. That doesn't mean, however, that he must die by the sword.

Did you want to stop yourself being on display to the world in the way your predecessor was?

My predecessor had his own mission. I am convinced that – after he took it up with mighty force, took all

[3] This was Martin Trimpe's celebrated PhD thesis: 'Macht aus Gehorsam: Grundmotive der Theologie des Päpstlichen Primates in Denken Reginald Poles (1500–1558)', submitted in Regensburg, 1982. See Vincent Twomey, *Benedict XVI: The Conscience of Our Age*, San Francisco: Ignatius Press, 2007.

of humanity on his shoulders as it were, and for twenty years bore the weight and the suffering of the centuries, he had proclaimed his message – a period of suffering belonged to that pontificate. And it was a unique message. People have seen it in this way. He's actually held so fondly by them as a sufferer. You come close to people's hearts if you are laid open. This was definitely his significance. However, I was convinced that one may not arbitrarily repeat this. It seemed to me after a pontificate of eight years it was not possible to cling on for another eight years.

You say that you sought counsel on your decision. Indeed, with your ultimate boss. How was that?

You have to lay out all your affairs before Him as clearly as possible and try not to see everything only in terms of efficiency or other criteria for resignation, but to look at it from faith. It was from precisely this perspective that I became convinced that the commission of Peter demanded concrete decisions, insights, from me, but then, when it was no longer possible for me for the foreseeable future, that the Lord no longer wanted me to do it and freed me from the burden, as it were.

There was a report that you had a 'mystical experience' which brought you to this step.

That was a misunderstanding.

Are you at peace with God?

Indeed, I really am.

Did you feel that your pontificate was somehow exhausted, that is was no longer moving forward correctly? Or that possibly the person of the Pope was no longer the solution but the problem?

Not in that way, no. I mean, I was certainly conscious that I was not able to give very much any longer. But that I was, so to speak, the problem for the Church, this was not and is not my view.

Did being disappointed by your own people play a role, feeling there was insufficient support?

Not that either. I mean, the Paolo Gabriele affair was a disastrous business. But first, I was not to blame – he was checked by the authorities and put in post by them – and second, one has to reckon with such things in human beings. I am not aware of any failures on my part.

Nevertheless the Italian media speculated that the true background to your resignation is to be found in the Vatileaks affair, not only in the Paolo Gabriele case, but also in the financial problems and intrigues among the Curia. Ultimately you were so shocked at the 300-page investigation report into these things that you could see no other way out other than to make space for a successor.

No, that is not right, not at all. On the contrary, the Vatileaks matter was completely resolved. I said while it was still happening – I believe it was to you – that one is not permitted to step back when things are going wrong, but only when things are at peace. I could resign because calm had returned to this situation. It was not a case of retreating under pressure or feeling that things couldn't be coped with.

In some newspapers there was even talk of blackmail and conspiracy.

That's all complete nonsense. No, it's actually a straight-forward matter. I have to say on this that a man – for whatever reason – thought he had to create a scandal to clean up the Church. But no one has tried to blackmail me. If that had been attempted I would not have gone, since you are not permitted to leave because you're under pressure. It's also not the case that I would have bartered or whatever. On the contrary, the moment had – thanks to be God – a sense of having overcome the difficulties and a mood of peace. A mood in which one really could confidently pass the reins over to the next person.

One objection is that the papacy has been secularized by the resignation; that it is no longer a unique office but an office like any other.

I had to accept that question, and consider whether or not functionalism would completely encroach on the papacy, so to speak. But similar steps had already been made with the episcopacy. Earlier, bishops were not allowed to resign. There were a number of bishops who said 'I am a father and that I'll stay', because you can't simply stop being a father; stopping is a function-alization and secularization, something from the sort of concept of public office that shouldn't apply to a bishop. To that I must reply: even a father's role stops. Of course a father does not stop being a father, but he is relieved of concrete responsibility. He remains a father in a deep, inward sense, in a particular relationship which has responsibility, but not with day-to-day tasks as such. It was also this way for bishops.

Anyway, since then it has generally come to be understood that on the one hand the bishop is bearer of a sacramental mission which remains binding on him inwardly, but on the other hand this does not have to keep him in his function for ever. And so I think it is also clear that the Pope is no superman and his mere existence is not sufficient to conduct his role; rather, he likewise exercises a function. If he steps down, he remains in an inner sense within the responsibility he took on, but not in the function. In this respect one comes to understand that the office of the Pope has lost none of its greatness, even if the humanity of the office is perhaps becoming more clearly evident.

Immediately after the announcement of your decision, the Curia went into their Lenten retreat, as always on Ash Wednesday. Was anything said about your resignation on retreat at least?

No, retreats are places of silence, of listening, of prayer. Of course it was part of the whole plan of the resignation for it to be followed by a week of silence, where everyone is able to work it out inwardly, or the bishops, cardinals and staff of the Curia at least. Because then everyone is taken away from external things and they interiorly face the Lord together. So it was good and poignant for me that, on the one hand, there was seclusion and silence and no one could disturb me – because there were no audiences, everyone was taken out of the hustle and bustle and we were very close on an inner level, all of us prayed and listened together four times a day with each other – but on the other hand everyone stood in his own personal responsibility before the Lord. So, I have to say the planning was very good. In retrospect I think it was better even than I was aware of at first.

Have you ever regretted the resignation even for a minute?

No! No, no. Every day I see that it was right.

So you haven't once yet said to yourself, maybe . . .

No, definitely not. It was considered long enough and spoken about with the Lord.

Were there any aspects to it which you had not thought of? Something which perhaps only became clear in retrospect?

No.

So you also considered whether or not there might in future be legitimate demands against a Pope calling for him to resign?

Of course you are not permitted to yield to demands. I therefore emphasized in my speech that I was acting freely. One is not allowed to go away if one is running away. One cannot submit to coercion. One can only turn away when no one has demanded it. And no one demanded it of me during my time as Pope. No one. It came as a complete surprise to everybody.

But it might have surprised you that through your resignation a turn to another continent was immediately inaugurated.

In the holy Church one must always be prepared for anything.

3

'I do not abandon the cross'

After celebrating your final liturgical celebration as Pope in office, and your departure from the Papal Palace, a new chapter began. Together with those closest to you – secretaries Georg Gänswein and Alfred Xuereb, as well as the four Memores sisters[1] – you moved first into the papal summer residence at Castel Gandolfo. Did you follow the conclave from there?

Of course.

How did you see it?

We had no guests, obviously, that much is obvious, and we had no sort of contact with the outside world, but we saw what could be seen on the television. We watched the evening of the election especially intensely.

Did you have any inkling of who your successor might be?

No, I did not at all!

No hunch, no suspicion?

No, no.

---

[1] The papal household under Benedict XVI included members of the Memores Domini, a lay association under vows of obedience, poverty and chastity.

Then how, taking leave of the Curia, could you promise your successor in spe *absolute obedience without knowing who it would be?*

The Pope is the Pope, regardless of who it is.

Bergoglio is rumoured to have been a favourite in the 2005 conclave as well. Was that the case?

I can't speak about that. [Laughs]

What were your thoughts when your successor stepped out onto the loggia of St Peter's Basilica? And dressed in white?

Well, that was his business, we were all in white as well. He did not want to have the mozzetta; that did not matter to me at all. I was very touched, however, that even before he stepped out onto the loggia he wanted to call me by telephone, although unfortunately he did not reach me, as we were watching the television. Also by how he prayed for me, that moment of reflection, and then the cordiality with which he greeted the people. That made the spark catch immediately, you might say. No one had expected him. I knew him, of course, but I did not consider him – so it was a great surprise to me. But that convinced me immediately, the way he prayed on the one hand, and on the other, how he spoke to the hearts of the people.

Where did you know him from?

From ad limina visits and correspondence. I grew to know him as a very decisive man, someone who in Argentina would say very firmly, this is happening and this is not. I had not experienced this aspect of warmth, the wholly personal connection to the people; that was a surprise to me.

Were you expecting someone else?

Certainly, yes, not anyone in particular, but another, yes.

Bergoglio was not among them, however.

No. I did not think he was among the more likely candidates.

Although they say, as mentioned, he was one of the favourites at the last conclave, next to you.

That is true. But I thought, that is past. I had not heard any more from him.

Were you joyful at the election result?

When I heard the name I was uncertain at first. But when I saw how he spoke with God on the one hand and with the people on the other, I was truly glad. And happy.

Once more, for the record: so one could not say that some knowledge or suspicion of who your successor would be had made your resignation easier?

No. The College of Cardinals is free and has its own dynamic. It is not possible to predict who will be chosen in the end.

Many things about Pope Francis are unprecedented. He is the first Jesuit Pope; he is the first to choose the papal name of Francis; and perhaps most importantly, he is the first Pope from the 'New World'. What does that mean for the global Catholic Church?

It means that the Church is flexible, dynamic and open, and that it is developing from within. That it is not frozen in old patterns, but that surprising things happen again and again. That it carries a dynamism which allows for constant renewal. What is so beautiful and encouraging, is that in our times most of all there are things that one would never have expected and that show the Church to be alive and full of new possibilities.

On the other hand, it was probably to be expected that South America would play a central role. It is the largest Catholic continent, and at the same time it is suffering the most and facing the most problems. It has bishops who are truly great men, and – in the midst of such trouble and suffering – a profoundly dynamic church. And so in some sense I think South America's day had come. The new Pope, though, is South American and Italian, so he represents both the intertwining of the new and old worlds and the inner unity of history.

With Pope Francis, in any case, the global Catholic Church is losing its Eurocentricity, or at least its Eurocentric tendencies will weaken.

It is clear that Europe can no longer take itself for granted as the centre of a global Church, but that the Church now truly appears in its universality with equal stature for all the continents. Europe retains its responsibilities, the specific duties it has. But faith in Europe is weakening so much that, on that basis alone, Europe cannot fully and solely be the driving force behind a global Church and behind the faith within that Church. And we are seeing new elements, such as African, South American or Filipino elements, bringing new dynamism to the Church which can reinvigorate the tired West, wake it from its exhaustion, from its forgetfulness of the faith. Particularly when I think of Germany – of the power of bureaucracy there, of how theoretical and political faith has become and how it lacks a living dynamism – which often seems as though it is nearly crushed by overweight bureaucratic structures, it is encouraging that other actors are asserting themselves in the global Church as well. In the end, they are missionizing Europe anew from the outside.

If one says the loving God corrects every Pope in his successor – in what ways are you being corrected through Pope Francis?

[Laughs] Yes, I would say, in his direct contact with people. That is, I think, very important. He is definitely a Pope of reflection as well. When I read *Evangelii gaudium*, or even the interviews, I see that he is a thoughtful person, who grapples intellectually with the questions of our time. But at the same time he is simply someone who is very close to people, who stands with them, who is always among them. That he is living in Santa Marta as opposed to the Palazzo is due to the fact that he wants to be among the people at all times. I would say that that is something one can achieve up there as well [in the Palazzo Apostolico], but it does show the new emphasis. Perhaps I was not truly among the people enough. And then, I would say, there is the courage with which he exposes problems and searches for solutions.

Your successor is not perhaps a little too boisterous, too eccentric for you?

[Laughs] Every person must have their own temperament. One person might be somewhat reserved, the other a little more forceful than one imagined. But I do think it is good that he approaches people so directly. Of course, I ask myself how long he will be able to maintain that. It takes a great deal of strength, two hundred or more handshakes and interactions every Wednesday, and so forth. But, let us leave that to the loving God.

So you do not have any problems with his style?

No. On the contrary, I approve, definitely.

The old Pope and the new Pope are living on the same patch of earth, only a couple of hundred yards apart from one another. You had said you would always be at your successor's disposal. Does he seek out your experience, your advice?

In general there is no reason to. On certain topics he has asked me questions, such as on the interview he gave in *Civiltà Cattolica*.[i] OK, I answer him, of course; I express myself. But all in all I am very glad that normally I am not brought into these matters.

So you did not receive Pope Francis's first apostolic exhortation – Evangelii gaudium – before anyone else?

No, but he did write me a beautiful personal letter which I received along with the exhortation, in his tiny handwriting. It is much smaller than mine. In comparison, my handwriting is huge.

Which is hard to believe.

Yes, very. The letter was very endearing, and so I did get his apostolic exhortation in a way that was special. And it was bound in white, as it normally is only for the Pope. I am currently reading it. It is not a short text, but it is a beautiful one, and grippingly written. Certainly not all of it by himself, but much of it is very personal.

Some commentators have interpreted this exhortation as a break, particularly because of its call for the decentralization of the Church. Do you detect a break from your Papacy in this programmatic text?

No. I, too, always wanted the local churches to be active in and of themselves, and not so dependent on extra help from Rome. So the strengthening of the local church is something very important. Although it is also always important that we all remain open to one another and to the Petrine Ministry – otherwise the Church becomes politicized, nationalized, culturally constricted. The exchange between the local and global church is extremely important. And I must say that, unfortunately, those very bishops who oppose decentralization are those who have been lacking in the kind of initiatives one might have expected of them. So we had to help them along again and again. Because the more fully and actively a local church itself truly lives from the centre of faith, the more it contributes to the larger whole.

It is not as though the whole Church were simply dictating to the local churches: what goes on in the local churches is decisive to the whole. When one member is diseased, says St Paul, all are. When, for example, Europe becomes poor in faith, then that is an illness for the others as well – and vice versa. If superstition or other things that should not occur there were to fall in upon another church, or even faithlessness, that would react upon the whole, inevitably. So an interplay is very important. We need the Petrine Ministry and the service of unity, and we need the responsibility of local churches.

So you do not see any kind of break with your pontificate?

No. I mean, one can of course misinterpret in places, with the intention of saying that everything has been turned on its head now. If one isolates things, takes them out of context, one can construct opposites, but not if one looks at the whole. There may be a different emphasis, of course, but no opposition.

Now, after the present time in office of Pope Francis – are you content?

Yes. There is a new freshness in the Church, a new joyfulness, a new charisma which speaks to people, and that is certainly something beautiful.

Two phrases from your departing speech in St Peter's Square stand out. The first was during your last Angelus*, when you stated: 'the Lord calls me to ascend Mount Tabor'. What did you mean by that?*

In the first place, that was set by the day's Gospel reading. But in this moment, the Gospel had received a meaning which was so concrete. It signified that now I was, as one might say, departing with the Lord, ascending out of the everyday of life to another height, where I am more directly and intimately together with Him; and, in doing so, that I was also relinquishing the throngs of people which had surrounded me previously, and entering into this new, greater intimacy.

It is also surely no coincidence that your last liturgy occurred on Ash Wednesday. It seemed as if you were saying: Behold, this is where I lead you: purification, fasting, repentance.

I did not choose that either. But in preparing, I did think about Ash Wednesday as well. That there would be a long liturgy to celebrate there. Normally it would have been in Santa Sabina, as that is the stational church, but in this case we moved it to St Peter's. And I did see that as quite fitting: that the last liturgy would be the beginning of the time of repentance, linked to the *Memento Mori*, the gravity of entering into the Passion of Christ – but also the mystery of the Resurrection. To have Holy Saturday on the one hand, writ above the beginning of my life, and on the other hand Ash Wednesday in all its meanings at the end of my concrete service – that was something that I reflected on in the first place, and yielded to in the second.

The second phrase of your farewell that sticks out was stated forcefully: 'I do not abandon the cross.'

Well, it had been said by some that I had climbed down from the cross, that I had done the comfortable thing. And that is an accusation that I had to expect, that I had to face inside myself before I took the actual step. I am convinced that this was not flight, and in no sense an escape from practical pressure – which was not there.

But nor was it an inner flight from the demands of that faith which leads man to the cross. It is instead another way to be connected to the *suffering* Lord as well, in the stillness of silence, in the grandeur and intensity of praying for the entire Church. So this step is not flight, not an attempt to escape, but in fact another way of remaining faithful in my service.

You did not stage some grand departure ceremony, but instead simply held a general audience.

If one were to celebrate that farewell, then that would truly be completing the secularization you mentioned earlier. It had to remain within the boundaries of what is part of spiritual service. In this case, the liturgy of Ash Wednesday and meeting the faithful in St Peter's square, joyfully and contemplatively in one. Although in that, the personal fate of the man is not what is central, but that he represents another. So it was absolutely right to face the Church as a whole again on the one hand, and on the other to interact with those people who wanted to say farewells. And to do this precisely not in the sense of a worldly celebration, but in that of meeting one another in the word of the Lord and in shared faith.

Then, when you flew off in the helicopter – that somehow felt like part of the whole dramaturgy of it, at least seen from the outside. You could say that that was the first time we saw the ascension of a living Pope . . .

[The Pope laughs]

What was going through your mind?

36

I was very moved. By the heartfelt goodbyes, and that colleagues [voice breaks] were in tears, as well. Then, above the house of Pastor Bonus there was a big banner saying '*Vergelt's Gott*', and then the bells of Rome . . . [the Pope begins to cry].[2] That did move me deeply. But in any case, floating above like that and hearing the bells of Rome, I knew that I should give thanks, and the fundamental feeling then was gratitude.

---

[2] '*Vergelt's Gott*' (*Vergelte es Gott*) is a Bavarian expression of gratitude to God. Literally it means 'may God repay you', and it invokes God to reward someone whose service or generosity cannot be rewarded by mere earthly means.

PART TWO

A Life in Service

4

Childhood and Parental Home

Holy Father, you went from being a child of humble circumstances to being the successor of Peter in old age. What ideas did you have of the Pope as a boy?

The then Pope, Pius XI, was for us the Pope *par excellence*. He was just the vicar of Christ, someone who stands infinitely beyond us, but at the same time is very near to us, because he is our common shepherd. We revered the Pope and loved him – and at the same time viewed him as being at an endless distance, infinitely far above us.

Did you have a favourite saint at this time?

I couldn't say. Of course I always liked my namesake, St Joseph, a lot.

As a child, did you have one of those childlike questions about God, for which one can find no answer, making one feel quite desperate?

No, because for me the world of faith was built very firmly and securely.

In a letter to the Christkind *you asked for a Missal, a set of green vestments for dressing up, and picture of the sacred heart.[1] You were seven years old, isn't this very unusual?*

[Laughs] Yes, but for us to participate in the liturgy really was from the very beginning a constitutive and noble experience; it was a world full of mystery, into which one wants to penetrate further. And playing at being a priest was a nice game anyway. That was still widespread then.

After your sister Maria and your brother Georg, you are your parents' third child. Were you the baby of the family?

Yes, of course.

They called you that as a child?

As a little boy they first called me 'Josepherl', but when I was about eight years old I said it couldn't go on; otherwise I'd live my whole life as Josepherl. From then on, I told them, I was to be called Joseph! This instruction was duly observed and complied with.

Were you a happy and uncomplicated young lad, or more of an introvert, being thoughtful early on?

At first, in Tittmoning and Aschau, I was a very funny boy. But later, somehow or other – I cannot give any reason for it – I became somewhat more thoughtful and

---

[1] Writing letters to the Infant Christ (*Christkind*) is an Advent tradition in Bavaria, where children ask for Christmas gifts. The interviewer specifies a particular edition of the Missal, the '*VolksSchott*' – a people's edition of the Missal in German produced by the Benedictine Anselm Schott at the end of the nineteenth century. See Joseph Ratzinger, *Milestones: Memoirs 1927–1977*, San Francisco: Ignatius Press, 1997, pp. 19–20.

no longer so merry. That changed. The war complicated everything.

The day of your birth, 16 April 1927, fell on a Holy Saturday. When, as Pope, you visited Turin and saw the Turin shroud, you cried out: 'This is the moment I've been waiting for.' This shroud is an image of Holy Saturday. It seems you had by then recognized this theme increasingly during the course of your life as the destiny assigned to you, this theme which formally endorsed you as you lay in the cradle.

Yes, I've always found it very pertinent. At that time Easter Night was celebrated on the morning of Holy Saturday, and I was baptized with the first baptismal water. That was something very dear to my parents' heart. They felt it was very meaningful and told me that from the beginning. An awareness of it has stayed with me to some extent. Both as a theologian and also in temporal events, which sometimes seemed very Holy Saturday-esque, it has been increasingly impressed upon me. I have also tried to understand it ever more deeply – actually as a title, something considered as a programme for my life.

Your words concerning this are very deep and touching.

Because it is not just something I thought up, but something bound up with the beginning of my existence, with the ground of my being, which I have not only thought my way into, but lived into as well.

As with Karol Wojtyla's father, your father Joseph Sr, a farmer's son and a policeman, had a very deep, masculine piety. Is this something your vocation is marked by, so to speak?

43

In some ways, certainly. On the one hand he was an incredibly pious man, who prayed a lot, was very deeply rooted in the faith of the Church, yet on the other he was a very level-headed, critical man, who could be quite negative towards the Pope and the bishops. The level-headed piety especially, which he lived the faith with and with which he was really imbued, all that was very significant for me.

Was there any particular event connected to his religious development?

That I don't know. In childhood he had a very good chaplain, who had clearly shaped him and had an impact. He spoke of him often. His teacher had, in turn, built up a boys' choir in which he sang. So the Church certainly became a lived experience for him.

Your father had no particular schooling to speak of?

He only went to the *Volksschule*,[2] but he was a man with reason who could think for himself.

Is it true that he wanted to become a priest?

He never spoke about it. He probably thought of joining the Capuchins as a brother.

From the Ratzinger family's farm at Rickering, a tiny village in the Bavarian forest in which your father was born, a striking number of vocations have come forth, directly and indirectly. There's the famous Georg Ratzinger, your great-uncle, who

---

[2] *Volksschule* usually refers to the minimum education required by German law.

was not only a priest but also made a name for himself as a Reichstag deputy. Then your father's siblings, Alois and Theogona, who were a priest and a religious sister respectively. In addition there is yourself and your brother Georg, and finally also a cousin, who is a priest to this day in Simbach in the district of your birthplace, Marktl. One could almost call it a family of priests.

Almost, yes. [Laughs] We got to know Uncle Alois well, the spiritual uncle, on holiday in 1937, or maybe as early as 1935. We also knew our aunt Theogona well, the religious sister.

Has it encouraged you on your own way that priests are in the family, like Uncle Alois, your father's brother?

That was normal then. The big farming families all had many children, so there was always a clergyman in the family.

Uncle Alois must have been a strange man.

Yes, he was a curious figure He was smart, but very unconventional. He was above all a great supporter of the German *Volksliturgie*.[3]

And he was anti-Nazi.

He was clearly that.

In the anthology Priests under Hitler's Terror, *two thick works with a list of priests from the Nazi era who resisted*

---

[3] The *Volksliturgie*, 'people's liturgy', was part of an early movement towards liturgical reform.

and were persecuted, it says that at the end of 1936 your uncle was reported by the president of the district because his congregation had sworn an oath to the Catholic Church. Were you aware of that as a young boy?

It was really clear to us that a clergyman must be against the Nazis. Our father was so against them you cannot imagine that anyone in the family would have supported them. Aunt Theres, one of my father's sisters, was particularly fierce against the Nazis. She had a house with several siblings in Osterhofen, with some ground on which the railway ran. When a train with Nazi top brass shot past on the train, she showed them the long nose [Pope makes a gesture, laughing]. They were enraged, but there was nothing they could do from a speeding train.

The year 1933 was declared a 'Holy Year' by the Church.[4] But in that year, of all years, Hitler came to power – the one who would bring death and terror to the world.

The date was set in advance, obviously. According to tradition the Lord was crucified aged thirty-three, and 1933 was a great Jubilee, which was also marked in Aschau where we then lived. At the same time, there was this triumph of evil hanging over us. But the inner world of our religion was so alive in us that, although it was certainly burdened by exterior events, it could not be destroyed.

For your father, who subscribed to the antifascist newspaper Die gerade Weg, it must have been a—

---

[4] The year 1933 was declared a 'Holy' or 'Jubilee' year by Pope Pius XI to mark the 1,900th anniversary of Christ's sacrifice on the cross.

It was completely terrible for him, yes. We children had a family life, a village life, which was still very Catholic-orientated. He was, of course, much more affected than us.

Your mother once worked as a seasonal cook in a pension; was that an issue at home?[5]

That was only after my father's retirement, because all three children were going to school and that had to be paid for. Even though I was boarding, the tuition was twenty marks a month. When she helped out at Reit im Winkl in 1938 the financial situation was particularly hard.

How was that for your father? He was probably the first house-husband in German history.

[Pope gives a laugh] It was a great challenge for him. He could only cook one thing, namely *Schmarren*.[6] Other than that he had to learn everything for the first time.

Did he have a problem with standing there in an apron?

He did it.

He even cleaned your shoes.

He had always done that, for the whole family actually. That was his department.

---

[5] A German 'pension' is a basic hotel, normally without a restaurant, roughly equivalent to an English Bed and Breakfast.
[6] *Schmarren* (literally: 'rubbish' or 'nonsense') is a basic meal of chopped-up pancakes, traditional to Swabia and Bavaria.

As a policeman your father was often moved about. Fourteen times in thirty-five years of service. Most of these were at his own request. What was going on?

I cannot explain it, but in the Ratzingers there is apparently a certain inner restlessness. I went hiking a lot . . .

Did he marry so late because of his many relocations as a police officer?

Yes. And yet also, I think, due to doubts about whether he would enter into an Order in some way.

And why did your mother marry so late?

That was probably also because of her employment circumstances.

Your mother was an illegitimate child. When did you find out about that?

That was actually quite early, in Aschau, although I didn't understand it at that time. It was as follows: as an official my father had to provide an 'Aryan certificate', to prove he and his wife were Aryans. For himself that was no problem, because the register of births was available. But mother came from South Tyrol;[7] there was a long, arduous correspondence between the pastor of Aschau and the municipality in Italy. It was thereby put on record that she was illegitimate. Nevertheless I didn't understand it properly until much later.

Did you need more of an explanation?

---

[7] South Tyrol is today a German-speaking province in the northernmost region of Italy.

Absolutely not. Because mother was convinced she didn't need to prove herself morally.

Did your mother ever find out who her father was?

Of course, the man who her mother then married was also really her father.

But the baker Reiger had not legitimized her at first. Why not?

That was a legal oversight. My mother was the first child of two. Even the second child, Benno, was premarital. They had already made their marriage vows, but were without a permanent residence. When they moved to Rimsting, where they had a bakery, he then married her. He thought the daughter was automatically legitimized when the parents marry. The mother was very strict, a hard woman; the father was kind and loving. He loved her very much – and she loved him too.

How is it for you? Did you find approval and love with your father?

I really did, yes. Already as a little boy. There was much geniality and warmth. Especially from April 1937, when he retired, we had many long walks on which he talked about his own childhood and youth. When my mother took on the position of cook in Reit im Winkl for financial reasons, and my siblings were no longer at home, we went for a walk every day. He was actually a novelist and always made up exciting stories. I think he enjoyed coming up with these tales, as the story would be continued next time. They were family stories. About a couple, how they become acquainted, everything that happens in the family; I would call them proper *Heimatromane*.[8]

How was your parents' marriage?

It was very good, although their temperaments were very different. Mother was genial, loving, warm-hearted, and not so rational. She liked to live on a whim, in the moment. In this regard their lifestyles were very different. There was a quarrel occasionally. There was a deep inner unity, so the quarrel would upset us, but we always knew that the essence of their marriage was intact.

Your father was strict, perhaps too strict you thought once. How would you comment on this strictness?

I must say he became more and more mild. With me he was no longer as strict as he had been with my older siblings. The strictness manifested in that he demanded punctuality and precision, that you were not allowed infringements on these things, and that he could scold you vigorously and give you a clip round the ear. This was at that time regarded as a normal way to bring children up. You knew that you had to keep order, the order of the faith, the order of the family, and law in general. He was a very law-abiding and honest man, and he ensured that one continued on this path. And yes, you could feel that it would not be taken lightly if you overstepped the mark.

---

[8] *Heimatromane* ('homeland' or 'pastoral' novels) are a genre of popular literature with a strong sense of place and regional identity.

You later made allowances for one of your professors in Freising for living according to 'uptight nineteenth-century piety'. You wrote verbatim: 'that was a breakthrough for me'. Was your father maybe also too strict in religion?

Put it this way: he had been particularly affected by a chaplain, of whom we've already spoken – an inherently good person. In this sense he had already been formed by nineteenth-century piety. Today, one would say that it was too strict sometimes. But you cannot compare the context then with today's context.

When you write about your childhood it mostly sounds romantic. You even imagined once that heaven could be likened to 'how life was in my childhood'.[9] Are you voicing a certain need for harmony there?

Certainly, yes.

Anyway, conflicts, fractures, difficulties are not a feature of your memoirs.

There was, of course, strife and suchlike in the family. We were completely normal people. It was not that everything was always harmonious. But the feeling of togetherness and happiness with one another has far outweighed that.

Was there no generational conflict, as had generally erupted in the 1960s?

No.

[9] In 2012 at an event in Milan, Pope Benedict XVI answered questions on the family, to one of which he said: 'I imagine heaven to be as my childhood was.'

You were admitted to the diocesan seminary at Traunstein after your older brother had already gone down this path. Was Georg an example to you?

In many respects, sure. He was simply a boy who knew what he wanted and had clear, decisive ideas. At the same time we were close from the beginning, we simply belonged together. Later we had theological discussions about all the questions which were then going round. I was only in the third grade of the Gymnasium when I entered the seminary. This was for a straightforward, practical reason: my father could not have paid if all three of us were at residential school at the same time. So I was granted two years at home, and that did me a lot of good.

Remarkably, your sister also continued to a secondary education. Was your father the driving force here too?

Yes. He wanted my sister to have a good education and good opportunities for work. Then, the Gymnasium did not fit the idea of a woman. There were two types of high school: the Lyceum, which was something more or less for noblewomen, and the household school, with stenography, typewriting, bookkeeping, English and so on. That was a solid education which gave her much joy.

Being a child when you started at Traunstein, you were more weedy than the others. Did you feel like an outsider?

Not really. When I entered the seminary, the world there was very new to me; that is how it was. But only for the first six months.

Your peers were impressed that very early on you seemed to know what you wanted, or what's what. In one of your reports from Traunstein it even says you had been 'rebellious'. Does this rebelliousness belong fundamentally to your nature?

It was that way a few times, yes. The third and fourth grade was somehow a time of rebelliousness, yes.

But not only then. There was the episode in the military, when the drill was going on, and the instructor – a real taskmaster – bellowed to all the recruits assembled before him: 'Who's holding out for longest, you or me?' And you stepped forward on your own and said: 'Us.' Ironically, it was the smallest, apparently the weediest, who gave the watchword. Later, too, this attitude was increasingly perceptible. For instance with your Habilitationsschrift,[10] in which you went against current scholarly opinion and particularly opposed a professor of dogmatics who was considered a leading worldwide authority in this discipline. So you were rebellious at this time too.

It is there, yes. The desire for contradiction, that's right.

In school you were called 'Hacki'. The school magazine Helios *wrote about you: 'As a person full of stark contrasts Hacki now stands in the limelight; however little he can do in sport, he is an intellectual man.' This edition comes from 1945, so intellectual pursuits were your thing very, very early on.*

Indeed, yes.

---

[10] The *Habilitationschrift* is a dissertation undertaken in German academia after the PhD thesis, enabling a candidate to qualify to lecture in a German university.

Your style of working was a distinguishing feature from the very beginning, with its fixed rhythm, through the regularity, the fixed daily schedule. When did this start?

That just happened after we were in Hufschlag.[i] Previously we were not given homework at school. In Hufschlag I spent the first two hours of the afternoon – or however long it took me, often just an hour – working. This then gradually extended. Anyway, it was clear to me that I should divide my time, so then I would really use the time allocated to work for that purpose.

As a schoolboy and as a student you were ahead of the others. Why was that?

One should not exaggerate. I particularly loved Latin and Greek and also learned Hebrew well. But hey, I was someone particularly given to these things, while others had less theoretical interests.

At fourteen you discovered literature, you translated Church texts from Greek and Latin.

More for fun than anything else.

Where did you actually learn the many languages? Surely one does not learn all those in school?

No, I'm not fluent in many languages actually.

Excuse me?

From 1942 to 1943 we had a year of Italian as an elective subject, but this was very often dropped. At least you learned a few minimal basics, but nothing more.

This then came only through practice, when I came to Rome. But I never properly learned Italian, so I'm never entirely sure about the grammar. We had a year of French at school. I tried hard to keep it up, but it was something of a meagre foundation. English I learned from vinyl records when I was in Bonn, but it always stayed very feeble. It looks as if I know as many languages as God, but this is not the case.

What did your parents say about their son's enormous talent?

Well, it wasn't so thrilling. I had good grades, but I had to work.

Was there a particular ambition, which, say, your father encouraged?

I wouldn't say so. Father gave much attention to making sure we were well schooled and orderly. But he did not want us to be anything 'great', and certainly didn't invest anything in that. He was pleased that we wanted to be priests. He was simply a man who really lived in the piety of the Church.

The vocation to the priesthood, according to your memoirs, 'naturally matured within me without any grand conversion experiences'. If there was nothing grand, were there little spiritual experiences, at least?

I would say it was my entering ever more deeply into the liturgy. Genuinely to recognize liturgy as the central point and seeking to understand it, together with the whole historical tapestry standing behind it. We had a teacher of religion who was writing a book about the

Roman station churches.[11] In a sense he used the religious instruction to prepare his book. Through him we learned the historical roots really well, very concretely. That was something that gave me real joy. With this I was then altogether preoccupied with religious questions. It is the world in which I feel most at home.

[11] The Roman station churches are churches in an ancient sequence where worship takes place through Lent and Easter in a set order for each day.

5

The War

At Easter 1939 you entered the diocesan seminary at Traunstein. A few months later, the Second World War began. Do you still remember the outbreak of war on 1 September 1939?

Yes I remember it well, because it involved the consequence that the seminary was immediately made a military hospital and from then on we went to school from home. Since the Austrian crisis of 1938 one knew war was coming. In this respect I remembered very well, as had been reported, that Hitler declared 'returning fire' at I don't know what time of the day.[1]

In wartime your father went to the farms in the area to ask for food.

He said that openly. We also knew which farms they were, where he could hope for something.

Catholic school pupils in Traunstein were menaced by Hitler Youth fanatics; they had to keep a low profile. There were

---

[1] Benedict XVI here uses the phrase '*wird zurückgeschlossen*', which were Hitler's exact words at 05.45 a.m. when he declared there 'was returning fire' from the German forces against the Polish military on 1 September 1939.

attacks on the diocesan seminary. For you as a child, weren't these threats from Nazis frightening?

Certainly. I mean, there weren't any real Nazis in our class, thanks be to God. So you didn't need to be afraid that one would be reported anywhere. But the atmosphere was oppressive overall. We knew that in the long run the Church was supposed to disappear. There was no longer supposed to be any priesthood. That was clear to us: I have no future in this society. The Nazi perspective was particularly dire for me personally, as sport was made a compulsory subject to finish school, and if you were not sporty you'd fail. At the same time we were always firmly convinced that Nazism could not last for long. My father was certain of this himself. We thought that the war would end quickly, because we believed that France and England were significantly stronger than the Nazis. This gave very great hope that it would not last for ever. But dread, a depression, was afoot. Then, when the first of our friends fell, we realized it was coming our way; then everything weighed more heavily on us.

Did your family know about the concentration camps? Did people speak of such things?

We knew that Dachau existed. The camp was opened at the same time as the so-called seizure of power.[2] If you heard that this or that person had been sent to Dachau, you were horrified. My father was a reader of Gerlich's *Die gerade Weg*. He knew that Gerlich [Fritz

---

[2] The 'seizure of power' (*Machtübergreifung*) refers to the period following Hitler's becoming chancellor of the Weimar Republic in 1933 in which the Nazis consolidated power and established a totalitarian state.

Gerlich, 1883–1934, whose newspaper *Die gerade Weg* is considered to have been one of the most important proponents of journalistic resistance to National Socialism] was slain or shot at Dachau. That terrible things were going on there, that we knew. The Jewish Question was not so pressing for us, because there were no Jews in Aschau nor Traunstein. That is, there was a timber merchant in Traunstein, but after he was thrown through a window he moved away the very next day. We didn't know any Jews personally. However, when we needed fabrics for sewing, my father had always sent for these from a firm in Augsburg, whose owner was a Jew. When the Nazis confiscated it and the new owner advertised that everything would continue as before, he said: 'No, I will not take up what one man has taken from another.' He never bought from this firm again.

When did you and your family find out about the gas chambers at Auschwitz and elsewhere, and about the mass murder of the Jews?

We listened to the foreign news broadcasts, we were avid listeners, but we heard nothing of the gas chambers. We well knew that it was going badly for the Jews, that they had been transported away, so you had to fear the worst, but I didn't know anything concrete until after the war.

Did you speak about it?

Yes of course. Father had always called Hitler a criminal, but that was a new, incomprehensible dimension which made everything seem much more dreadful.

After being released from the anti-aircraft unit you went to do Reich labour service in Burgenland. You described it in your memoirs. Where exactly was it?

In Deutsch Jahrndorf, which is on the border of Slovakia–Hungary–Austria, very close to Pressburg. From where we were you could see the Citadel of Pressburg, so Bratislava. The Hungarian border was right next to us. We had to work the harvest on the paprika fields. Our accommodation consisted of primitive barracks, five or six, and there we were grouped by size. The biggest were in barracks 1, I was in barracks 4 or 5. People weren't so big then, as I was classed as medium height. We were about fifteen per barracks, sleeping on bunk beds.

You had to travel out every day to erect a 'southeastern wall'?

The first fortnight, maybe even three weeks, was only drills. Then the war moved closer. In the morning everyone had to pick out a bike from a big crowd of bicycles. You had to pay attention so you could get one as quickly as possible. Sometimes you had bad luck and got landed with a bad one. We cycled to the site, yes, and there you simply dug around.

With the famous spade you have told of.

I was a bad shoveller, to be sure. There were some capable ones, farm lads, who could do it properly. The *Führer* certainly didn't benefit from me.

In mid-December 1944 you had basic military training in Traunstein. One of your peers related that a forty-kilometre

*march in gas masks had been arranged. Quite a few broke
down, but you withstood it well.*

Forty kilometres is an exaggeration; it was thirty, I
believe. We did indeed carry gas masks, but we didn't
have to wear them much. I was always good at walking, because we walked from Hufschlag to school in
Traunstein.

*From mid-January 1945 – you were seventeen years of age –
you were transferred again and again to other locations in the
vicinity of Traunstein. At the beginning of February 1945 came
the exemption from duty. What caused your absence?*

There was no great disease. I had a whitlow, an infec-
tion on the finger. My whole thumb had gone horribly
sceptic and hurt terribly. Then the doctor, who was
more of a vet [laughs], cut into it without anaesthetic.
He made it worse, not better. Maybe he meant well,
and it was positive for me. He certainly got me signed
off from duty.

*And you were never involved in hostilities. At the end of April,
the beginning of May, according to your memoirs, 'I decided to
go home'. That sounds very terse. In reality that was desertion,
punishable by death. Were you not aware of this?*

I did ask myself that afterwards. I knew that if I was
standing there at my post when the allied forces arrived
I would be shot immediately, so things could actually
only end badly. Still, I really can't explain why I so
blithely went home, that is, how naïve I was.

*What did your father say about it? You were a deserter,
after all.*

Father, the whole family, immediately received me joyfully. I have spoken about how, when I came home, two religious sisters – 'English girls'[3] – were sitting at the table and studying the map. And as I entered there in uniform, they thought, 'Thanks be to God, a soldier is here, now we're protected.' They didn't think that the exact opposite was the case.

SS men immediately turned up at your home, but there were no consequences, though your father hurled abuse at them. Shortly before the end of the war you were taken into custody by soldiers of the US Army. You could only take with you a notepad or, at least, something to write in . . .

A book, a proper book.

What did you note down in it while a prisoner of war?

Everything imaginable. So situations, but also proper essays about subjects which I knew about because they had been studied at school. Then I tried my hand at Greek poetry and what have you. So nothing worthwhile, mere reflections of my days.

Some of your classmates were traumatized by bad experiences in captivity. You were in a camp for fifty thousand prisoners at Ulm. How was that for you?

It was very difficult. At first we didn't get anything to eat for two days. On the third day we only got an American ration; it was the first time in my life I had ever seen chewing gum. Then, when we arrived at our

---

[3] Those in the order named 'Congregatio Jesu' were called the English Girls as they had been founded by the Englishwoman Maria Ward.

designated place, we were always outdoors. The first fortnight went well, because there was lovely weather.

That means you slept on a mat in the open air?

I slept on the bare soil; there were no mats.

Without a blanket?

Without a blanket. As long as it was warm, it didn't matter.

It was not high summer, it was May, June. You're actually more robust than one would think.

[Laughs] When you're young and you're hoping that it won't last for ever . . .

And when the rain came?

That was completely awful. A few tent communities had been set up, but I didn't belong to any of them; the 'big chief' of our block then admitted me into one, but they made it so clear to me there that I was not welcome that I left. Eventually there was a corporal who had a very little tent – the German tents were indeed very small. He was nice and said the two of us could make a little tent community together. Later, another fellow came along with a larger, Czech tent and we were then better accommodated. He was dismissed before me and gave it to me to take home. He later came to Hufschlag and collected it.

You had to carry the tent with your luggage on the way to Munich by foot?

Yes, yes. [Laughs] But it was the hunger that was terrible. We got a cooking pot full of food only once a day. In addition to this, theft was widespread. When the two of us had dug out a trench for our tent – dug ourselves in – I dug a little compartment and put bread in it. I went to sleep and when I awoke the bread was gone. One was so hungry in any case. But what was important to me was that these communities organized lectures and suchlike. Then it was not so terrible for me.

The decision to become a priest continued to mature in captivity. Did Hildegard of Bingen's biography, Das lebendige Licht *by Wilhelm Hünermann, which you had already read by the age of fourteen, also play a role in this?*[4]

My brother read this book to us aloud in the evenings at home. I wouldn't say it was decisive for my vocation to the priesthood, but it was certainly an edifying read which helped us. I tried later to have at least a basic knowledge of her. The figure of Hildegard always followed me; it was always engaging, always precious to me. But I haven't managed to undertake the deeper engagement with her that I had planned.

What did your mother say about your priestly vocation? Did she firmly express it herself? Like, for example, Don Bosco's mother, who said: 'If one day you doubt your vocation, then take off your cassock. Better a poor peasant than a bad priest.'

Ah, that's nice. That would also correspond to my mother's attitude. She didn't say it in this way. She was

---

[4] Wilhelm Hünermann (28 July 1900–28 November 1975; born in Kempen, Germany) wrote a number of saints' lives as novels. *Das lebendige Licht* (*The Living Light*) was first published when Joseph Ratzinger was fourteen, in 1941.

pleased that my brother and I went in this direction. But she was of the opinion that if it is not our own path, then it is much better that we go away from it. Provided that was borne in mind she was always joyful about it, but it was a reserved joyfulness because she knew that things can go wrong too.

6

Student, Curate, Lecturer

On 3 January 1946, you began your studies in Freising. You were sent on your way on the train with your brother Georg and another student from Traunstein, Rupert Berger. What did you have in your luggage?

[Laughs] I had clean clothes of course, just what you need to live. Maybe a second suit too, and a few books, but very few, as we didn't have any books.

You didn't have any books at home?

We did, sure, but none that could be needed there.

Presumably the train to Munich was crowded: refugees, former soldiers, peasant women . . .

You were crammed in terribly. The trains were jam-packed but you still just got on. That was normal then.

What was going through your mind as you started this journey?

It was exciting, of course, to see how it would be. In the first place the seminary itself, but above all the lectures, the professors. We had a friend, a classmate of my brother's, who had already gone to Tübingen in November. The university lay in the French zone of occupation; they immediately opened it again and the theological faculty could continue working from the beginning. He told us about it enthusiastically in the Christmas holidays. He said everything was different from the Gymnasium and so forth. He was completely enraptured. We also knew, however, that most of the house in Freising was still occupied by foreign prisoners.

How was it when you arrived in Freising?

It was a dream come true, finally to begin and enter into the world of academic study, theology, and the companionship of future priests. We went there with great excitement, but also with great openness and willingness, with a great hope. I still remember my first encounters, which are now hardly worth sharing. As we climbed the cathedral hill, the person first approaching us was someone who would later become Professor Fellermeier. We marvelled at this young, noble, gentleman, who was very formal. The exterior conditions there were a bit arduous. The majority of the seminary was still a foreign military hospital. Only a part of it was freed up for us, where we were housed somewhat primitively.

The 'Holy Mountain' must have actually been quite to your liking?[1]

---

[1] It was on a mountain near Freising that St Corbinian erected a Benedictine monastery and school in 716. On this site stands today's cathedral, along with the seminary and university.

It certainly was. The cathedral alone was captivating, it was stunningly beautiful. It had definitely begun well. First of all we had a retreat straightaway, led by Professor Angermair, the lecturer in moral theology at the university; it was very good. He was a fresh, new thinker who particularly wanted to take us out of the cramped piety of the nineteenth century, and into the open. You sensed the new mood, and it was a breakthrough for me, so to speak. Accordingly, your curiosity then grows while you're in university, even if everything wasn't quite so convincing there.

Even the site of Cathedral Hill, with its views of the Alps, is enchanting. Then there is this incredible church, the cloister, the crypt. Everything is charged with the great tradition of Bavarian Catholicism, with the prayer and the experience of believers down the centuries. The high spiritual atmosphere really is palpable.

It was still burdened by the presence of the military hospital and the fact we were therefore only allowed to use the house within limits. But nonetheless it was overwhelming to see the square: Johanneskirche, the university, the cathedral, and there behind the Benediktuskirche, the seminary and seminary chapel, which were also wonderful. And so, despite the intrusiveness – where the atmosphere of war was still somehow in the air – there was a joy that we were now together. The being with one another, the encountering each other, the companionship, was subsequently something deeply moving for me in my consciousness.

In your memoirs you particularly single out the great liturgical festivals in the cathedral, but also the silent contemplations in the seminary chapel.

Both were very important. The cathedral with all its splendour, so a church with a beauty that is over-whelming. Then the music in the cathedral was very beautiful. Although the chapel was small – it had to be enlarged so that everyone had a seat; we kneeled right at the back and were quite far away – nonetheless, with its altarpiece and its inner atmosphere, it had a vitality which was really tangible.

In later life you have increasingly withdrawn to go on retreat in monasteries, to the Benedictine monastery at Sheyern, for example.[2] Which retreats and spiritual exercises have you found particularly valuable?

The first retreat, in 1946, was particularly moving. Then, naturally, the retreats before our diaconal and priestly ordinations – to recollect, to pray about this great moment – penetrated the soul deeply. Because you trod all the inward paths again, gathered everything together inwardly, opened it all up and once again asked: 'Am I worthy? Am I capable?' That was very, very moving for me. Following priestly ordination, every year we had a three-day compulsory retreat. Of these, a retreat led by Fr Swoboda – a Viennese Camillian, of the Order founded by Camillus de Lellis[3] – made a lasting impres-sion, for he preached the retreat with freshness, vigour and decisiveness, but also a great competence. Then Hugo Rahner [the brother of the theologian Karl Rahner] also gave a retreat. I must say that was a little depressing.

[2] For many years Joseph Ratzinger made an annual retreat to the Sheyern Abbey in Bavaria, which houses a Benedictine community.
[3] St Camillus de Lellis (1550–1614) founded the Order of the Carmillians in 1582.

Depressing?

I don't know, maybe because his illness had already become apparent to him.[4] Anyway, for him somehow faith was not only joy. He was, more than anything, a weary believer, I had that feeling. The following year it was a priest of St Michael; he gave a joyful retreat[5] which we went away from feeling pleased and happy. He was a completely simple man. But he radiated joy. He also told us some amusing things. For example, that when nothing came to mind for the sermon in St Michael's, he would put on Rupert Mayer's hat [Rupert Mayer was a Jesuit and preacher in Munich, an opponent of the Nazis, d. 1945 and beatified in 1987]. Then ideas would suddenly come to him. Finally, there were the retreats I made in Sheyern as bishop every year, always alone, so not with a guide, which were invariably moments of spiritual recollection and opening up.

You also had a retreat firmly booked in 2005, but you were elected Pope just before it. Why Sheyern?

We had once visited there, but I didn't get to know the monastery intimately. In my first days in office as bishop, Tewes [an auxiliary bishop in Munich] said to me that I was now to go to Sheyern for a little while to seclude myself. There I thought to myself, here you are. The rural expanse, the great forests, and the unrestrained stillness and openness, the simplicity of the abbey and the steadiness of the rhythm – all that really spoke to me.

---

[4] Hugo Rahner suffered from Parkinson's Disease.
[5] The Pope Emeritus could be referring here to a Jesuit priest from St Michael's Church in Munich.

With the beginning of your studies in Freising you belonged to what was literally the first year of priestly formation after the inferno of Nazi dictatorship and the world war. Can one say that the depth of your experience of the brownshirts' dictatorship has fundamentally influenced your work?

Yes, one *must* say that. We experienced a time in which the 'new *Reich*', German mythology, Germanism, were the great things, and Christianity was something contemptible, particularly Catholic Christianity, because it was Roman and Jewish. Through the war you grasped this more strongly from the directives. You knew that every day you were endangered. As long as you had to fear that the Third Reich could win, it was clear that everything, all of life, would then be destroyed. Nevertheless we always knew that could not be, Hitler winning. However, the swift victory over France, the rapid advance into Russia, the victory of Japan which immediately destroyed the whole American fleet, these were moments in which one was unsettled. Now to be living in freedom again, to be in an era in which the Church can come forth afresh, have questions put to her and is being sought out, this was lovely to see. At the same time you experienced the old Nazis suddenly fawning over the Church. Our former French teacher, for example, an awful Nazi and Catholic hater, now came up to the priest in Haslach bringing a bouquet of flowers, and there are other similar stories . . .

You seldom address the topic of the Third Reich and Hitler's fascism in your writings. Why is that?

Well, the eyes are always looking to the future. And it was not specifically my topic. We had the experience within us, but to reflect further on it historically or philosophically was something I never saw as my task. For me the important thing was to conceive the vision for tomorrow. Where are we today? How will things proceed with the Church? How will things proceed in society?

But the question of the shared responsibility of the people, or the involvement of the Church in the Nazi system, was unresolved. These issues came to be interpreted differently in later years.

We experienced it differently, I must say. Now it is made out that the whole Church had been an instrument of the Nazis. We experienced the Church as being harassed – I will not say persecuted – and as a place of resistance. I remember well how, after the war, suddenly nobody wanted to have been a Nazi any more; as our priest said: 'It gets to the point where you end up saying the only Nazis were the priests.' Everyone laughed, it was a joke. No one could imagine that happening, because everyone knew that the Church was the only force that had held out. Sure, there was no big, active resistance or revolutionary things going on. But it was completely clear that after the war the Catholic Church was first in line to be eliminated by the Nazis, and that she was only still tolerated because they needed all their forces for the war. The notion that the Church might somehow be participating did not occur to us. This notion was only constructed later.

But can you not also say, as you put it, that the Church had generally been a place of resistance? There was such involvement, even by bishops, which was the case to a far greater extent in the Protestant churches.

There were these 'German Christians', who no one knows about any more, who were completely dominant.[6] It's true that my father sometimes grumbled because Cardinal Faulhaber was not more clear in his opposition to the Nazis, but he was nevertheless a witness against them. The documents of the Gymnasium in Traunstein show that the Nazis said: 'The spirit of Faulhaber rules the Seminary' – that means the anti-*völkisch* spirit and so on.[7] Faulhaber was the epitome of what the Nazis detested. My father felt that the bishops had to be more explicit. Well, there were different temperaments, but we never had the feeling that the Church would join in. The incompatibility was already shown in the programmatic book *The Myth of the 20th Century* [by Alfred Rosenberg, leading ideologue of the Nazi Party]; this was the ideological basis, and it was absolutely anti-Christian.

So the reason you did not address this question was simply that it wasn't your topic? I mean, it was certainly a major social issue which came up again and again.

It was, of course. But it was not my task to work on it intellectually.

Did Fr Höck, Rector of the Seminary at Freising, talk about his internment as a priest in the concentration camp at Dachau?

---

[6] The so-called 'German Christians' were a movement founded in 1931 which attempted to blend German Protestantism and National Socialism and aimed for the full Nazification of the German Protestant churches, and had a Nazi installed as *Reichsbischof* (Reich bishop) in 1933.

[7] The *völkisch* ideology is a set of views which considered the German race ('*Volk*') to have pseudo-divine properties, and this deeply influenced Nazism.

Yes, once for the whole afternoon. He made a sketch on the wall and explained everything in detail.

Were there discussions about the 'White Rose', about the resistance?[8]

One knew of it and spoke about it. We were proud of the 'White Rose'. As schoolchildren in Traunstein we heard what they did in Munich, and our whole class showed sympathy. Everyone said: 'They're plucky.'

You were later closely associated with the sister of Professor Kurt Huber, who was a leading member of the 'White Rose'.

She was a noble person of deep faith, a woman of sincerity.

One of the key readings of your student days was the book Der Umbruch des Denkens, *by the moral theologian and social ethicist Theodor Steinbüchel.*[9] *How did you see yourself as a young man? Modern, critical?*

Well, I didn't want to operate only in a stagnant and closed philosophy, but in a philosophy understood as a question – what is man, really? – and particularly to enter into the new, contemporary philosophy. In this sense I was modern and critical. Reading Steinbüchel was very important to me, because he – also in the book *Die philosophischen Grundlagen der christlichen Moraltheologie* – gave a comprehensive overview of contemporary philosophy, which I sought to understand

[8] The White Rose was a Catholic Nazi resistance group led by staff and students at the University of Munich.
[9] *Der Umbruch des Denkens. Die Frage nach der christlichen Existenz erläutert an Ferdinand Ebners Menschdeutung,* Regensburg: F. Pustet, 1936.

and inhabit. Unfortunately I could not go as deeply into philosophy as I wanted, but just as I had my questions, my doubts, and didn't simply want to learn and take on a closed system, I also wanted to understand the theological thinkers of the Middle Ages and modernity anew, and to proceed from this. This is where personalism, which was in the air at that time, particularly struck me, and seemed to be the right starting point of both philosophical and theological thought.

At this time another key text came along, Henri de Lubac's Katholizismus als Gemeinschaft.[10] *You write that de Lubac 'was leading his readers out of a narrowly individualistic and moralistic mode of faith and into the freedom of an essentially social faith, conceived and lived as a we'.[11] This faith differs from that of your childhood, of your origin. Was there a conflict?*

No actual conflict, no. It was an extension, a broader horizon, but for me it definitely had an inner identity with what we learned in piety as children. Because it was always clear then that the love of neighbour is something important, and that faith simply wants to understand the whole. In that regard it was, so to speak, the discovery of what was actually meant, but could not be seen in our catechism theology. Here I really have an inner continuity, and also joy thereby, that one was

---

[10] This is the German translation of *Catholicisme: les aspects sociaux du dogme* (Paris, 1938), translated by Hans Urs von Balthasar. This work was also translated into English as *Catholicism*, by L. Sheppard and E. Englund (London: Longman Green, 1950), and later reissued as *Catholicism: Christ and the Common Destiny of Man* (San Francisco: Ignatius Press, 1988).

[11] Seewald here quotes Ratzinger, *Aus meinem Leben*, p. 69, given here from the English translation *Milestones*, p. 98. For Ratzinger's discussion of the '*we*-structure' of the faith, cf. *Principles of Catholic Theology*, San Francisco: Ignatius Press, 1987 [1982], pp. 15ff.

able, after a period of somewhat sterile formulations, to see the faith anew, continuing, and even being admitted into contemporary life. In that sense it was certainly a breakthrough, but not a discontinuity.

So no conflict with your father, with his ideas or his piety?

No, because my father was a thoroughly realistic man. He was very interested in Catholic social teaching. He was concerned with things like Catholicism as a social reality. In this sense the ground had already been prepared inwardly for this new direction.

In your longing to open things up and learn something new, did you ever discuss such matters with your father?

No, we didn't do that. Discussion about these matters wasn't his thing. But he knew that we had good guidance, and that we would not forsake the spiritual foundation, prayer and the sacraments. That was decisive for him.

Regarding the beginning of your studies at the university, you once said, 'when I began to study theology, I also began to be interested in intellectual problems, and these because they revealed the drama of my life and above all the mystery of truth'. We've already spoken about this in *Salt of the Earth*; at that time you felt it would have been expressed a little 'pompously'.[12] To ask you here once again, very directly: what was that 'drama of your life'?

Well, dramas surrounding what I can do with life. Should I become a priest or not? Will I be suitable for

---

[12] cf. Joseph Cardinal Ratzinger, *Salt of the Earth: The Church at the End of the Millennium*, San Francisco: Ignatius Press, 1997, pp. 59ff.

it or not? And overall: Why am I here? What is wrong with me? Who am I?

Again, how did you see yourself?

We were forward-thinking. We wanted to renew theology from the ground up, and thereby form the Church in newness and vitality. In this respect we were lucky that we lived in a time in which both the youth and liturgical movements had opened up new horizons, new paths. Here we wanted to press forward with the Church, so that, in precisely this way, she would be young again. At that time we all had a certain contempt for the nineteenth century; it was fashionable then. So neo-Gothic and those rather kitschy figures of saints, the narrow, somewhat kitsch piety and over-sentimentality – we wanted to overcome all that. We wanted a new era of piety, which formed itself from the liturgy, its sobriety and its greatness, which drew on the original sources – and was new and contemporary precisely because of this.

Were you an existentialist?

I haven't read Heidegger much, but I've certainly read some and found it interesting. One revisits this philosophy, these concepts, with a certain tension. As mentioned already, I wanted out of classical Thomism, and Augustine was a helper and guide with this. In this connection it was worthwhile entering into a living conversation with contemporary philosophy. But I've certainly never been an existentialist.

You now felt you had developed enough for that 'conversation with Augustine'. As stated in your memoirs, it was a conversation that 'I had already been attempting for a long time in different ways.'[13] *Sounds very mysterious.*

[Laughs] Well, when you're young you linger over doing something, then you think you can manage it. I wasn't familiar with the complexity, 'about which purer and greater scholars have written', but I thought: we are young people, we have a point of entry. From this certainty that we are able to build the world anew, I was fearless before great things. It is true that I came across Augustine early in 1946 and read a few of his works. The personal struggle which Augustine expresses really spoke to me. Thomas's writings were textbooks, by and large, and impersonal somehow. That said, there is of course a personal struggle standing behind them, which you only discover later. Augustine battles with himself, and indeed continues to do so after his conversion. And that is what makes the subject compelling and beautiful.

At this time you liked to go to the theatre and the opera in Munich. What particularly interested you there?

Fundamentally, the representation of human life, of human affairs. I was particularly fascinated by *Der seidene Schuh* by Paul Claudel, or also *Des Teufels General* by Zuckmayer, and the opera *Dialoge der Karmelitinnen* by Francis Poulenc, the libretto of which is based on the play with the same name which Georges Bernanos wrote after the original *Die Letzte am Schafott* by Gertrud von Le Fort. I also remember a very beautiful performance of *A Midsummer Night's Dream* by Shakespeare, and

---

[13] *Milestones*, p. 98.

a piece by Paul Claudel about Queen Isabella, which had black-and-white drawings of Spaniards and Indians which today must seem astonishing.

Staying with art: do you have a favourite painter, a favourite picture?

I've always really liked the Dutch painters; alternatively, our Bavarian baroque artists.

With the Dutch painters, van Gogh?

No, the old ones. Rembrandt, for example; he was in our youth a myth in itself. But above all Vermeer van Delft. My sister gave me a very beautiful picture by him.

What are your favourite pieces by Mozart?

There's a clarinet quintet that I really like. Then the *Coronation Mass*, of course. The *Requiem* I've particularly enjoyed. It was the first concert I heard in my life, in Salzburg. Then *Eine Kleine Nachtmusik*. We tried to play that on the piano as a duet when we were children. *The Magic Flute*, naturally, and of the operas I would still say *Don Giovanni*.

One or two favourite pieces by Johann Sebastian Bach?

Yes, Bach – the B Minor Mass is particularly dear to me. I've asked my brother for a new recording of it for Christmas. Then the *St Matthew Passion* of course.

Now, I have to ask about Karl Valentin. What did you like so much about the Bavarian comedian and maverick? In the summer of 1948 you made a pilgrimage from Fürstenried to his grave in Planegg. A walk of at least thirty kilometres.

I didn't feel that was such a long distance. I was just always good at walking. [Laughs] At that time I had a colleague, Walter Dietzinger, who has since died. He had a fundamental intelligence, was a slightly curious type of man, but he was also a great admirer of Valentin. With him I felt this enigmatic, strange, grumpy serenity; I understood his particular sort of enigmatic humour, as, yes, somehow significant. I realized that you can also come to reflect about things which you can laugh about.

There is Valentin's beautiful saying, 'Today I will pay myself a visit; I do hope that I'm at home.'

I know it well. Hitler even once shook hands with him and said: 'Mr Valentin, I have very often been able to laugh heartily with you.' Then Valentin responded: 'I've never been able to laugh with you yet.'

Really?

Yes, yes, really.

Gottlieb Söhngen was an influential teacher of yours in Munich. What were your first impressions of him?

In the very first lecture I was spellbound. As a native of the Rhineland he had a natural rhetoric, and he had a way of speaking that would immediately draw someone in to the topic. He mainly addressed problems. At that time in the historical disciplines and in exegesis, a certain positivism prevailed. But Söhngen didn't want somehow to construct an impressive, self-sufficient academic edifice, but instead to ask: How is this real? Is this possible for me? That was what moved me.

Were you also close personally?

At that time you were, of course, always deferential to the professors; it was a whole other world. My brother and I were such little country folks. But in the first oral exam I got closer to him personally.

Did he consider you his protégé early on?

No. He couldn't have done.

Why not?

Well, because at first I was still just a young lad, and I had barely begun looking into things deeply.

But you were his de facto protégé. Did that put pressure on you?

I didn't see it as such myself. No, I was glad that I was able to work, that I understood what things were at issue for him, that I was now gradually coming closer to glimpsing theology as a whole, and that it seemed I would be able to try doing something theological myself.

Can one say that it was Söhngen who was your real theological teacher?

You can say that, yes, you must say that. I mean, the others meant a great deal to me of course. I was certainly also shaped by learning dogmatics with Schmaus. Then

Pascher, naturally, primarily through his lectures. Three times a week he held these so-called 'Points Sessions'. In these he came out of himself and spoke freely for up to an hour. Overall, the faculty truly influenced me. The highlight was of course Söhngen; he moved me the most, and he was the one through whom I discovered and recognized what theology is.

What was the defining feature of the 'Munich School'?

It was defined by the fact that it was completely biblically orientated, working from Holy Scripture, the Fathers and the liturgy, and it was very ecumenical. The Thomistic-philosophical dimension was missing; maybe that was its real benefit.

Söhngen belonged to a group of theologians who thought there was no dogmatic basis for the Assumption of Mary into heaven. Can one say that Marian devotion and Maryology were not particularly incisive for you at this time?

I was Catholic, of course, and therefore the May devotions, the reverence of Mary during Advent, the month of the Rosary and simply the love of the Mother of God pertained to us, but it was not as deep, not so strongly present emotionally, as is the case in classically Catholic countries like Poland or Italy. Bavaria is certainly also a classically Catholic land, but the emotional vitality was not as great as elsewhere. Devotion to Mary influenced me, but together with Christocentricity, and taken up into that.

Although your father was surely a great devotee of Mary.

And my mother. It was very present in my family and belongs to the fullness of my catholicity. For instance, from childhood on we set up a May Altar in the village. But my theological formation was very Christocentric and patristic, from which Mariology is not absent but it has not yet gained inner vitality. In this respect, pious practices, and what we learned theologically, had not yet intertwined with each other.

Did Söhngen have contact with Romano Guardini?

They certainly knew each other, but I don't think they were closely connected.

Did you feel, as a few others did, that Guardini was not a proper theologian?

[Laughs] I would not dare to say that now. He [Söhngen] did quote Guardini at one juncture in his book *Die Einheit in der Theologie.*[14] In the notes he said: 'I can no longer find the quote and I ask that that be considered a testament to a living relationship with its author.' I would say he certainly knew him, but they were not very close. In contrast, Pascher and Schmaus were very closely connected to Guardini.

Did you get to know him personally?

Personally, not so well. The first encounter of a personal sort was in Bogenhausen. He lived in Bogenhausen. He called us one day, a Friday evening, and asked whether he could celebrate on Sunday, and the parish priest—

---

[14] Gottlieb Söhngen, *Die Einheit in der Theologie. Gesammelte Abhandlungen, Aufsätze, Vorträge,* Munich: Zink, 1952.

That was the parish priest at Blumschein, where you were curate?

—the priest was completely speechless. Guardini wants to celebrate with us, to hold the last supper! He was flabbergasted. Guardini was a rather reserved man, but very simple and lovable. My brother knew him better, because he was curate at St Ludwig then, and met him every Sunday. In 1956 we went with a friend to Franconia, where an uncle lived, one of my mother's brothers. So when we passed through Rothenfels, we thought, now we have to go up to the castle where Guardini had been bringing young people for decades. It was of course highly fitting that Romano Guardini walked out of the castle gate just then. We go up there, and what's going on? Guardini walks out of the castle gate! [Laughs loudly] It was like a dream. He showed himself to be most delighted. 'It's strange who you bump into just because you're there!' Then we had a little chat. But that was one of the few encounters of a personal sort.

Rupert Berger, one of your fellow students, says that you also occasionally experienced Guardini together as students, when you had to jostle for space at one of his lectures in the packed auditorium at the university.

Certainly, yes. One of the first books I read after the war was a little life of Jesus – not a big work – by Guardini.[15] I found it very fascinating, after other lives of Jesus had seemed to me to be boring and trite. In this sense he was certainly on my radar.

[15] Romano Guardini, *The Lord*, Washington: Regnery Publishing, 1952 (reprinted with an introduction by Joseph Ratzinger in 1996).

Your studies now finally came to an end, and also your practical formation for the priesthood, during which, among other things, you had to handle dolls in order to learn how to baptize a baby properly.

There were practical subjects – pastoral theology, liturgy – where you learned to read the mass, administer the sacraments, or even hold catechesis sessions in school. We tried to learn that in groups, overseen by the Vice-Rector. And we got to grips with it so slowly.

Perhaps you didn't take it at all seriously, because you thought: 'I won't be this sort of priest anyway. I will certainly be a priest, but in order to be something other than this.'

No, no. I already had a conscious intention: 'I must not become a professor. I am ready and willing to become a pastor.' That was an important inner struggle for me. It was for me completely vital that, if the bishop doesn't want me to take that path, then I will just become a pastor.

You give remarkable evidence in your memoirs, though, that you sensed early on that God wanted something from you that could only be realized if you were a priest.

Indeed. I mean, somehow I had the knowledge that God wanted something from me, expected something of me. And it became increasingly clear to me that this something was tied up with the priesthood.

But this was obviously about something secondary, something which goes beyond the priesthood.

Yes, well, He demands something specific of every human being. I was convinced that He also wanted something from me. However, I also already had the thought that this would be something along the lines of theology. But that was not defined in a narrower sense.

So you handled this baby doll at the font with full solemnity then?

Yes, yes, of course!

And were you adept at it or not so much?

I was, for once, less clumsy than usual. Then, in my first year as curate in Bogenhausen, I performed many baptisms, because there was a birthing clinic in our parish, where I had a few baptisms every week.

Singing lessons are a feature of priestly formation. Apparently you were taught by a former opera singer?

Yes, Mr Kelch. He has since died. He lived to be over ninety.

Was your sense of pitch a problem? Did you work on it?

Yes, a little. But, well, there's not a great deal that can be done about it.

The following motto is written on the invitation to your first mass: 'We don't rule over your faith, we serve your joy.' How did that come about?

As part of a contemporary understanding of the priest-hood, not only were we conscious that clericalism is wrong and the priest is always a servant, but we also made great inward efforts not to put ourselves up on a high pedestal. I would not even have dared to introduce myself as 'the reverend'. To be aware that we are not lords, but rather servants, was for me something not only reassuring, but also personally important as the basis on which I could receive ordination at all. So the statement on the invitation expressed a central motivation for me. This was a motive I found in various texts in the lessons and readings of Holy Scripture, and which expressed something very important to me.

Your students say that they were able to observe, over decades, that your celebration of the Eucharist was never stale, but that you wholly devoted yourself to the full change in the elements on every occasion, as if it were for the first time.

Well, it is so exciting that one meets it repeatedly. I mean, it is something completely extraordinary, that the Lord is here himself. That this is no longer bread, but the body of Christ – of course this permeates someone.

On your time as a curate at Bogenhausen: are experiences from this period incorporated into your essay 'The New Pagans and the Church'?

That year was actually the loveliest time of my life. But I also experienced this new situation as something very dramatic, especially as regards leading religious instruction, since I had forty boys and girls before me who somehow participated well, but I knew that they heard the opposite at home. 'But Daddy said you don't need to take it so seriously.' It was palpable that, although everything institutional was still there, the real world had already shifted away from the Church to a large extent.

Weren't you saying something a bit crazy in this essay? I mean, after the war it was a time in which the Church appeared to be flourishing again, firmly establishing itself institutionally. Then someone comes along and says a new paganism is developing.

Yes. But it was so obvious. We had a good youth ministry. But they all suffered inner conflict, too, because in their religiosity they somehow stood at odds with, were alien to, their own world.

'The New Pagans and the Church', published in 1958 in the journal Hochland, *was your first high-profile act of provocation, of which many more were to follow, right up to being in the office of Peter. What were the reactions to it like?*

They generally tended to be negative, unfortunately. Strangely enough, it was alleged that in this article I had taken up a position against the CSU.[16] This was a one-off, though. Furthermore, it was rumoured that I had expressed something heretical. In Freising, where I was when the article was published, there was consternation. I had already been called to Bonn. Our colleague Scharbert, an Old Testament scholar who was taking his post-doctoral qualification in Bonn and had good connections there, told me they were also a little dismayed. One wonders whether it was right for them to have called me to Bonn. In Munich the main issue was that Cardinal Wendel was also aggravated. But he said to me later that although he had heard it was very alarming, he would never have passed judgement on

[16] The Christlich-Soziale Union in Bayern or Christian Social Union in Bavaria, a political party which has led the state government of Bavaria since its founding in 1946 until today, except between 1950 and 1953.

me – that is rejected me – on the basis of one article. It was comical; I have to say that I had no idea then what could disturb people so much. But in any case, it caused a commotion.

The article was an early wake-up call, an urgent call to recognize the signs of the times. How was it in terms of positive reactions?

They were some, of course. Primarily from the actual *Hochland* circle around Franz Josef Schöningh, who was not only the editor of *Hochland*, but was also one of the founders and the editor of the *Süddeutsche Zeitung*. The article was considered an important contribution.

With this article, did you also provoke an article by the writer Ida Friederike Görres in the Frankfurter Heften? *Görres wrote, in 1946, about the disillusioned everyday lives of many Catholics, and about the alarming state of the ecclesiastical institutional apparatus.*

That article was very famous. It was being discussed everywhere at that time. In Freising it was met with great indignation. I certainly knew what was in it, but I hadn't read the article itself. What had inspired me was the experience of the concrete Church, as I had encountered it beforehand as a curate. Somebody then invited Mrs Görres to Freising to give a lecture in the seminary. Cardinal Faulhaber decided: This woman is not speaking in a seminary!

You got to know Mrs Görres in 1970 and sustained an extended exchange of letters with her, and she probably often—

I met her in person as well. I took her funeral too. She had read *An Introduction to Christianity* and was very enthusiastic and happy about it, because here was a young theologian, a young generation, that portrayed Christianity faithfully. On the one hand she was very critical of the nineteenth-century forms of piety. But when the post-conciliar breaking away from the faith led to a new situation, she then took a very strict position – and she was happy to have found a young theologian in this book who was both modern and faithful. She wrote to me immediately and later visited me in Regensburg.

Initially, your appointment as lecturer in the seminary at Freising followed, with your first lectures dealing with the Sacraments in Pastoral Theology, among other things. At the same time you took on the leadership of a youth group. Hardly anyone knows you were also a student chaplain from 1955 to 1959.

At the technical university in Freising there was a faculty of agriculture and brewing – the 'Oxford of brewing'. There were Chinese students, people from all parts of the world were there; for example, someone from Cuba who was enthusiastic about Castro's revolution. Back then you could still be enthusiastic about it, or perhaps even had to be so. That was very rewarding for me. First, I had a monthly lecture evening, further I was a regular guest of the student organizations. I also had a little fund then, to be able to help students in emergency situations. They were very likeable young people; I experienced many beautiful things with them.

Did you sit in the confessional during those three years?

Of course. Every Saturday. For two hours on average.

What did you hear there?

It was mostly seminarians that came. I was particularly popular with them, because I was very generous somehow. [Laughs]

Does the date 21 February 1957 mean anything to you?

This was the day of my public habilitation lecture, which together with the post-doctoral thesis is necessary to qualify for holding an academic-level teaching position. My post-doctoral thesis had been sent back for improvements to be made, on the basis of a negative report by the second examiner, Schmaus; the second version was then accepted. But the mood was extremely tense, so I was really quite uneasy before this lecture. I proposed a historical theme for the lecture. Normally the faculty always accepted what was proposed. But it was said to me that, because I was qualifying in dogmatics, I must deal with a theme from systematic theology. I only had a couple of days to prepare this thing. I was fully occupied with my own lectures in Freising at the same time. I was very tense because I knew that certain elements within the faculty would listen to me with suspicion, and had essentially decided negatively already. My failing seemed inevitable. According to the established procedure, the primary supervisor, in my case Söhngen, had to speak first: that was expected to be amicable. The co-examiner, Schmaus, had already made it clear he would be presenting a less amicable point of view. But suddenly a dialogue sprang up between Schmaus and Söhngen, who hotly debated with each other inside the lecture hall. It was an extraordinary situation.

Your parents lived with you then. You had brought them to Freising. Were they in the audience?

My brother was there, not my parents. I wanted to spare them that. They stayed in Freising. I was present for the discussion, because the discussion should have been with me. In principle the professors do not debate with each other, but with the candidate. Then we waited in the corridor until the announcement of the decision: my brother, the preacher Pakosch von Sankt Ludwig, and whoever else was there. It seemed to go on for an eternity, and well, there I could prepare myself for the worst.

Which then did not occur.

After a long wait in the corridor I was informed that I had passed. The drama thus ended, even if it still had a psychological effect on me. Beforehand, I had indeed been standing on a precipice . . .

During that time did you fume against God, or make a vow that you promised to fulfil in the event of a good outcome?

Neither. But I prayed much and pleaded earnestly to the loving God for him to help me. Especially for my parents' sake. It would have been a disaster if I'd had to throw them out onto the street.

However, you also spoke of the profound experience which came from the trauma of your habilitation – that this test 'was healing for me humanly, and followed a higher logic'.[17] *What did you mean by 'higher logic'?*

Well, I had attained my doctorate very quickly. If I had quickly and easily passed again, people's awareness of that would have been too strong to enable me do anything meaningful, and there would have been an imbalance in my self-confidence. And so I was made very small on this occasion. That does someone good: to recognize once again, yes, one's utter poverty and to stand there not like a great hero, but rather as a lowly candidate who stands on the precipice and thus must reconcile oneself with what one then does. In this regard the logic was simply that I needed a mortification, and that it was somehow justified – in this sense justified – that it came to me.

Does this mean that you were inclined towards an inflated ego, or even egomania?

I mean, after gaining my doctorate, which was considered illustrious, the Rector immediately said that he hoped he would see me as a colleague in the seminary. Then I was just a hopeful youth. [Laughs] I was indeed always in the hands of Schmaus in the seminary. If he could not be present he entrusted me to take his seminars. That was very nice and encouraging, that I belonged to those figures from whom one hoped something would come.

And that went to your head?

No, it wasn't like that, but then one needs humiliations.

Humiliations?

[17] Milestones, p. 113.

94

I believe that it is dangerous for a young person simply to go from achieving goal after goal, generally being praised along the way. So it is good for a young person to experience his limit, occasionally to be dealt with critically, to suffer his way through a period of negativity, to recognize his own limits himself, not simply to win victory after victory. A human being needs to endure something in order to learn to assess himself correctly, and not least to learn to think with others. Then he will not simply judge others hastily and stay aloof, but rather accept them positively, in his labours and his weaknesses.

Is there actually still a copy of this thesis, with the critical notes by Schmaus in the margin in all their glory?

No, I threw it away. [Laughs]

Back then?

Yes, back then.

In anger?

I burned it.

In the oven?

Yes, in the oven.

After the acceptance of your thesis, you were at first appointed as a lecturer, then finally as a professor.[18] *You write in your*

---

[18] Peter Seewald here uses the word *Privatdozent* for lecturer, which is roughly equivalent to a visiting or associate lecturer in the UK, or an adjunct lecturer in the US; then *außerordentlichen Professor*, which is roughly equivalent to a senior lecturer in the UK, or associate professor in the US.

memoirs that this did not pass by without being preceded by 'some sniper shots from disgruntled quarters'.[19] *What did you mean by that?*

Apparently there were people who wanted to prevent me being appointed as a professor, and who denigrated me in my ministry. It happened like this: I attended an appeal hearing, at which a senior civil servant dealt with me very condescendingly, so I felt that he had been informed about me from somewhere. He said: 'How long have you actually occupied the professorial chair?' I said: 'Since 1954, so three years; I'm now in the fourth year.' Then he answered: 'Well, we probably have no other choice but to appoint you. Better someone than no one.'

What's that about?

He didn't produce any rationale. He simply entered the proceedings and wanted to play at being an official.

What were the actual grounds on which you were denigrated?

That I would just be incapable or something. I don't know.

In your memoirs you mention that your relationship with the Archbishop of Munich, Joseph Kardinal Wendel, was not wholly without ongoing complications.[20]

That was another matter again. I was at first denigrated by him as heretical etc., because of *The New Pagans and the Church*. But at this point it was about something

---

[19] *Milestones*, p. 112.
[20] See *Milestones*, p. 120.

else. Around this time, the end of 1958, the pedagogical academy in Munich-Pasing was being academically upgraded to university status. Until then the professors were not yet habilitated. But those in Munich had, in the megalomania which they certainly had, contrived to have Pieper installed as professor of philosophy. Those in charge had been persuaded by the cardinal's staff that I must take on the new theology professorship, so that the discipline of theology was represented well enough to withstand philosophy. Having both Pieper and me was for them the right thing to do. And the cardinal, who had little understanding of the German academic world, found that marvellous and said to me: 'You are taking on the professorship at the pedagogical academy and not in Bonn.'

That sounds like a really interesting option, with the connection to an excellent philosopher like Josef Pieper.

It was nevertheless a pedagogical academy and not my calling. I said: 'I can't do it.' He, however, insisted on it and would not release me to Bonn. It is a German tradition that a priest is automatically released if he receives a call to an academic post in a university. Then there was a rather complicated exchange of letters between us. In the end he did it, with some reluctance.

You put yourself at odds with your bishop's instructions?

Not that. I simply didn't immediately accept his first request. There was, as I said, a clear tradition in Germany that when someone is called to a professorial chair, he is released for it. Also, the cardinal hadn't straightforwardly rejected that, but had said: 'I have an important thing for you to do'; he had been misinformed about the state of affairs. Furthermore, I was secure in the knowledge that I would have been unsuitable for this position. Because in a pedagogical academy one is teaching future teachers who are not theologians, one must always make one's work interesting at a general level. That would not be my thing.

And how were you able to convince him?

There was a difficult and toilsome exchange of letters. It was probably the vicar general, Fuchs – who treated Wendel's manoeuvre with scepticism from the outset – who broke it to him gently that the tradition in Germany is always to release a priest called to a professorial chair. In any case, the bishop said to me one day that he did not like this matter, and especially didn't like the *Hochland* article either, but he did not want to hold me back and had granted me release.

Very early on, while still in Freising, your preoccupation with Protestantism began. Significant ecumenists have come from among your students. What attracted you to this?

Here, what I inherited from Söhngen was decisive. Söhngen came from a mixed marriage; that was an existential problem for him. His lectures were never only about the Catholic tradition, but rather always in dialogue with Protestantism too, particularly at that time with Karl Barth. From the outset, dialogue with Protestantism was part of my theological studies. Therefore I had in Freising already conducted a seminar about the Augsburg Confession [*Confessio Augustana*, the founding confession of the Lutheran Church]. As such, it was a matter of course that ecumenism was always an element of my lectures and seminars, and therefore my students would occupy themselves with it.

On the cathedral hill of Freising you got to know a representative of mystical Hasidism through learning about Martin Buber. Was this your first encounter with Judaism?

I would say so, yes.

What was it in Buber that so fascinated you? Later you even had a recording of him on vinyl.

I revered Martin Buber very much. For one thing he was the great representative of personalism, the I–Thou principle that permeates his entire philosophy. Of course I have also read his complete works. He was a bit fashionable at that time. He had newly translated the Holy Scriptures together with Rosenzweig. His personalistic viewpoint and his philosophy, which was nourished by the Bible, were made fully concrete in his Hasidic tales. This Jewish piety, completely uninhibited in faith and simultaneously always standing in the centre of the concerns of this time, his mode of having faith in today's world, his whole person – all this fascinates me.

You also read Hermann Hesse; for example, Steppenwolf *and* The Glass Bead Game.

I read *The Glass Bead Game* when it was published. That was in the early 1950s, I think. I read *Steppenwolf* in Regensburg, so in the 1970s.

Steppenwolf *was a favourite text of the hippies in San Francisco. What attracted you to it?*

It was the unstinting analysis of declining humanity. It is an analogous image to what is happening with people today. It was how the roots are laid bare in this book, the whole problem that really pervades someone. With *The Glass Bead Game* – I was still very young then and actually in a sheltered world at home – the idea moved me that, at the end, the protagonist has to start off again, that he goes away again. He is the great master of the glass bead game, but there is nothing final. There is a magic spell living within every beginning; he has to begin again.

7

Theological Apprentice and Star Theologian

The call to Bonn changed everything. In your memoirs it sounds as if there was a sigh of relief, a new-found freedom. You are also living alone for the first time. That is, not quite alone. Whose idea was it that your sister Maria came along?

Hers and mine. It was clear that I needed a housekeeper, and this was the best solution, rather than me starting to search for someone.

Not everyone would like having their siblings so close.

We were only three. In this respect we were innately very close.

Maria also accompanied you to your other places of work, even to Rome, before she died in 1991. She was, so to speak, the woman at your side. How much did she influence your life and work?

I would say it wasn't in the content of my theological work that she influenced me, but through her mode of existence, through the path of her faith, and her humility. Simply in the atmosphere of the shared faith in which we had grown up, which grew with us and held firm through time. The Council simply adopted this faith and renewed it, but it has remained persistent. I would say she was influential on the overarching mood of my thinking and being.

At first, you lived with students at the Albertinum theological hall of residence. Later, you had an apartment on the Wurzerstraße in Bad Godesberg.

The area had a big advantage: it was two minutes from the tram stop. So I could board a tram every quarter of an hour and travel on it right up to the university entrance. With the Rhine railway one could continue to Cologne. It was also a few minutes from the Rhine; one could go to the Heart of Jesus Church and other places by foot, the most beautiful walks.

You like to walk anyway.

Quite. There was a doctor in the building, who I didn't need in any case. There was a pharmacy opposite, but I didn't use that either. Two minutes away was a bank branch, which was already very convenient because the manager would memorize the account numbers of all his regular customers. When I came in, he would say immediately: 'Your number is so-and-so'; that was ideal.

What did you do first with your spare time? Did you go to cafés? To restaurants? Or didn't you have any free time at all?

Yes, well, first I've always walked, morning and evening. Professor Hödl and his sister lived next door, and a secondary-school teacher; we often ate together there and listened to records, played games together, Ludo and suchlike. In that sense we were certainly kept busy.

The perception that you are absolutely unsporty must be corrected. You rode a bicycle lots, not only as a child and young man, but also as a professor.

Yes, that's right, in Münster and then also in Tübingen and Regensburg.

Also in Munich, as archbishop?

No, I didn't dare. I've never ventured to be so unconventional.

And you have walked a lot.

A great deal, yes.

How and where do you most like to reflect on things?

At the writing desk, or if I have to think something through thoroughly, I lie on the sofa. There one can think things through steadily.

You always had a sofa nearby?

I always need a sofa.

You gave your inaugural lecture on 24 June 1959. The lecture hall was crowded. Stage fright?

No, I had written a good lecture.

You were remarkably self-confident.

Perhaps that's overstating it, but I knew the lecture was fine; in that sense I didn't need to be nervous.

Considering the well-known photo from Freising, where you are nonchalantly leaning on the lectern, propping your head on your hands, you were generally very much at ease.

That photo isn't typical. Overall I certainly also spoke with expressive gestures. Only occasionally, when a less intense passage came, did I adopt such a posture.

The subject of your inaugural lecture was 'The God of Faith and the God of Philosophy'. Was that set out in advance?

I produced it myself. It came about like this: as a student I had read a lot of Pascal. Gottlieb Söhngen had given a Pascal seminar, and had of course read Guardini's Pascal book, in which *Memorial* is particularly emphasized.[i] *Memorial* is about the 'God of faith', the 'God of Abraham, Isaac and Jacob', as a contrast to the 'God of the Philosophers'. It was very fashionable to condemn the Greek heritage as an aberration, an erroneous imposition onto Christianity. Instead, people wanted to seek the original substance of the Bible, the living God of Abraham who speaks to human beings, speaks to their hearts, and by doing so is wholly other, compared with the God of the philosophers.

One of your fundamental themes from the outset.

Yes, a question with which I was also then strongly confronted by Augustine. Augustine had not at first been able to start with the God of Abraham, Isaac and Jacob. He had read Cicero enthusiastically, particularly the philosophical speeches. There is in these certainly a keenness for the divine, for the eternal, but no cult, no point of access to God. He looked for that, knowing 'I must go to the Bible', but he was so appalled by the Old Testament that he said 'it is not safe'. He felt the contradictions very intensely, and indeed to the disadvantage of the God of Abraham, Isaac and Jacob, because these stories seemed to him to be unbelievable and frivolous. He turned his attention to philosophy, then fell into Manicheism, and only after that discovered what would remain his modus operandi for the rest of his life: 'In the Platonists I learned "In the beginning was the Word". In the Christians I learned, "The Word became flesh". And it is only thus that the Word came to me.'[1]

That means, for Augustine, it was not that these two approaches worked against each other, but that they essentially belonged together?

This fascinated me. I came to the conclusion: of course we need the God that has spoken, the God that speaks, the living God. The God that touches the heart, that knows me and loves me. But he must be accessible somehow to the mind. The human being is a unity. And what has nothing at all to do with the mind, but rather takes its course alongside it, would then not be integrated into my whole existence, it would remain some kind of separated element. 'How is it, really?' I asked myself. Here the God of faith, there the God of the philosophers. Does one cancel the other out, or do they belong together in reality? The Greek philosophers did

---

[1] See Book VII of Augustine's *Confessions*, Oxford: Oxford University Press, 1991, pp. 121f.

not want this Abrahamic God. Conversely the Old Testament originally knows nothing of the God of the philosophers. I then saw the way for each to lead to the other, in which Alexandria is their place of meeting. So I was, well, simply fascinated by this existential theme, which is about the question of 'What actually is my faith? How does it sit within the whole of my existence?'

According to your memoirs, your first semester at Bonn felt like 'one ongoing honeymoon'.[2] What did you mean by that?

On the one hand I lectured in philosophy of religion during this semester – 'What is religion, considered philosophically?' – on the other hand, the concept of theology: 'How is theology grounded?' What should it do? What is its role, so to speak; its inner rationale? These were the two sets of lectures that I had to give. Both touch on the central issue: 'How can the study of theology in a university be at all justified?' Does it fit in the contemporary university? Or is it a foreign body which is randomly standing still in some medieval prehistory and must actually be excised?

Would that then also include: what can one say philosophically about religion?

The concept of theology was a theme which I had already worked out somewhat in Freising, but I didn't need to have too much to do with it. I'd also already read some philosophy of religion in Freising, but I went about it again entirely from scratch. This gave

[2] *Milestones*, p. 118.

much delight both to me and to the students, so it had a sizeable, lively popularity. On the one hand, I was experiencing now the adventure of thinking, of knowledge, of advancing towards and entering deeply into things. On the other hand, I was sensing the popularity, the responses of the theologians, and that really was something to be celebrated. That people recognized the same things as I forged ahead, that I was really doing what I would inwardly most like to be doing, and that the students felt the same way and came along with me. I saw that I can give young people something: and then that this something develops further in ongoing dialogue with one another.

You've called this an 'atmosphere of renewal'.[3]

Yes, correct. It was all of that in the beginning. The University of Bonn had been destroyed in the war, and had just been rebuilt; the library was still incomplete. So the sense of renewal was pretty much evident. You had a sense that you could begin afresh after the war, and also examine the new situation afresh according to the faith. The Federal Republic was still young, and in this sense life was at a starting point. The feeling that a new beginning was afoot, in the faith, in the Church and in the state, and that we were able to contribute to it, was vivid and pleasing.

Did you work much in the library?

The university library had just been rebuilt again. We had a seminary library anyway, and I was there a lot.

[3] *Milestones*, p. 120.

As seminary director I could also buy books there. When the university library was reopened, in 1961 maybe, then I happily went there because they had the modern system of electronic issuing. That was something completely new for me, to order books and then they immediately appear.

Did you sit at your books late at night?

No, no, I was never one to work at night, not at all.

You write in your memoirs of a large audience, who 'reacted enthusiastically to the new tone they thought they could hear in my words'.[4] Your lectures were packed. Very soon you enjoyed the reputation of being a new, rising star in the theological firmament. How did you develop your style? Did you model yourself on anyone?

In Munich we had of course grown up with a modern philosophy. Certain professors had taken us to pastures new and opened them up for us. I had taken this mood on internally, and tried to perpetuate it according to the possibilities at my disposal.

Söhngen as role model?

In some way, certainly. Of course I could not imitate him. I mean, he was from the Rhineland, and I am through and through Bavarian. He was a great source of inward stimulation and a role model for a style of thinking, but not directly a figure I was about to imitate.

[4] *Milestones*, p. 115.

You invented the system of holding colloquia to supervise your doctoral students, in contrast to one-to-one supervision.

I certainly supervised my doctoral students personally and spoke individually with them. But I had the feeling that here was a group of people who were walking a path with me, who belonged together, who should also learn from each other, so that we could then all learn with and from one another. Therefore I concluded that every individual receives more along the way in cooperation with others than would be the case if going it alone.

All the comments on your students' work are written in pencil.

[Laughs] I had always done that. As a young lad I wrote in pencil and then stayed with it. The pencil has an advantage in that one can erase things. If I write with ink, it is written.

Did you also write with a pencil as Pope? Like with your Jesus book, for example?

Always, yes!

Never with a pen?

No.

In this little handwriting, which—

—has grown smaller over the course of time. But that is a process that happens to others, I believe.

It is striking that your friends and close colleagues in Bonn are mostly very controversial, maverick people, who rubbed the authorities in the Church up the wrong way. You obviously knew no fear of guilt by association?

That time was different. Only later was there separation between those who rejected the Magisterium and went their own way, and those who said that theology can only be done within the Church. Then, everyone was still aware that theology obviously has its own freedom and task, that it cannot be completely servile to the Magisterium, but we also knew that theology without the Church would be theology in name only, and would no longer have any meaning. I was considered someone who is young, who opens new doors, treads new paths, so then persons who were just plain critical came to me.

Like Hubert Jedin, for example, or Paul Hacker. The historian of the Council, Jedin, was half-Jewish, and found protection from the Nazis in the Vatican State. The Indologist, Hacker, was a former Lutheran.

Jedin's path is very interesting. He was considered a historian with his own, free identity, the opposite to one who was simply subservient to the Magisterium. But when he saw that people were stepping away from the Church, he became a staunch defender of ecclesiasticism. Paul Hacker was again a very particular character, who could argue. He was a bighead, an enormous head, but an explosive head with it.

Is it correct that after objections from Hacker you changed an article about naturalism which was to be printed in a Festschrift for Söhngen?

Yes, I really don't remember the content, but it is correct, he was an influential man. You could really discuss things with him. In the first place he had an incredible gift for languages. He spoke eighteen languages perfectly and reached a level of perfection in Sanskrit that meant Indians came to study Sanskrit with him. So he was a great master, someone with an unbelievably broad education, someone who knew the Fathers, knew Luther, and had mastered the whole history of Indian religion from scratch. What he wrote always had something new about it, he always went right to the bottom of things. One could only really learn from that, and sometimes argue of course.

Once, your students complained that you would only talk about Hare Krishna and suchlike in your lectures.

No, no, I've never spoken about Hare Krishna, but I have dealt with the myth of the god Krishna, which demonstrates astounding parallels to the history and character of Jesus, and is of great importance for interreligious dialogue. I had to lecture on the history of religion, and in that context I included a big section on Hinduism. It was very helpful then that I knew Hacker; I also got literature from him. In general, only the philosophical aspect of Hinduism was represented, whereas I was of the opinion that one must enter into the cultic and mythical aspects too. On the whole it was received very positively by the students.

Did it fascinate you?

Certainly, yes. And I'm glad that I did it then, because when interreligious dialogue came on the scene I was already somewhat prepared.

Your friendship with Hacker, they say, was also full of tension. Did you end up falling out?

I wouldn't say so. During my time in Regensburg, when he had become extremely critical of the Council, I wrote to him once, saying quite sharply that it's not so bad. But we understood each other. He knew that we were both – especially him, but me too a bit –very strong-headed, and were able to clash at times, but we certainly wanted the same thing.

Once he complained that all his money was being drained by telephone calls . . .

That might well be. Of course he didn't only telephone me.

Is it true that you took Hacker's text Gedanken zur Reform der Kirche *to the Council, on his insistence?*

No.

In it he speaks of a pseudo-ecumenism and warns of a 'protestantization' of the Catholic Church. He made the reproach to you that your Mariology is murky.

He reproached me many times, which is possible and proper among friends. As a convert he was initially very critical of Rome. But he increasingly turned away from that. Instead he was always very critical of Rahner, and tended towards one-sidedness, to the extreme. He always remained stimulating. But one does not have to see everything as he saw it, unconditionally.

Heinrich Schlier was another of your close colleagues in Bonn. Under Hitler he renounced every encroachment of the regime, and was a member of the Protestant 'Confessing Church' (in opposition to the 'German Christians', who were loyal to the regime). In 1942 he was banned from publishing anything. After the war he came to Bonn and took the professorial chair for New Testament. When he converted to Catholicism in 1954, it was a scandal of the first order, for he was a protégé of the leading Protestant theologian Rudolf Bultmann. His former colleagues no longer accepted him, and among Catholics acceptance was patchy. Schlier had to relinquish his professorial chair at the Faculty of Protestant Theology, but he remained an ordinary professor. His writings include a profession of faith in the Catholic Church, in which he justifies the path to Catholic faith with three other Protestant theologians. They say that he had the greatest influence on you. On the one hand he was a historical-critical biblical scholar, on the other, he was completely spiritual.

I would say he was not a uniquely big influence on me, but he certainly had quite an influence. I also really valued him as a human being. He was, as mentioned, innately Protestant and a member of the Bultmann school. He revered Bultmann to the last and learned a great deal from him, but outgrew him and went far beyond, and was, as he said himself, Catholic in a typically Protestant way: meaning 'Scripture alone'. His celebrated critical interpretation – the famous commentary on Galatians, the commentary on Ephesians, and one on Romans – is marvellous. And at the same time he was just a completely spiritual person. You've got that right. With him, the synthesis of historical–critical and spiritual is unique.

Who is Sophronius Clasen, with whom you also made friends in Bonn?

He was a Franciscan. At that time there were four major colleges run by religious orders in the Bonn vicinity, where really good people were taught. The Franciscans in Mönchengladbach, the Dominicans in Walberberg, the Divine Word Missionaries in Sankt Augustin, and the Redemptorists in Hennef-Geistingen. The Redemptorist patristic scholar Joseph Barbel was an outstanding man. The Divine Word Missionaries were famous for their history of religions research, and produced their own journal. The Dominicans produced the German edition of Thomas, and were ever so famous. The Franciscans had the journal *Wissenschaft und Weisheit*. Sophronius Clasen was there, professor of medieval studies or dogmatics, a great connoisseur of thirteenth-century theology and a Bonaventure specialist. He read my book on Bonaventure and came to visit me. Thus our friendship came about.

Can one consider these years as a golden age of German theology?

Yes, in many ways, even in terms of this circle of four institutions alone. These were no 'home butcheries'[5], as people used to say then. Here were really properly qualified people, from whom one could learn. The faculty itself had something to offer: there was Jedin, Klauser, Schöllgen, and many others. In this respect there was great blossoming. There was an awareness that we were living through a moment to which we had something to say.

If one views Cologne and Bonn together, you found yourself in the Catholic religion's centre of power, and at the political centre of the young Federal Republic of Germany, with

---

[5] 'Home butcheries' refers to unaccredited, dilettantish houses of study.

Konrad Adenauer as the first Chancellor and his counterpart, the SPD politician Kurt Schumacher.[6]

One can say that. Adenauer regularly travelled past our house when he came from Röhndorf and took the ferry over the Rhine. A few of our colleagues knew President Heuss very well. I have never attempted to make policy, but the awareness that Germany was shaping itself anew, and seeking a new form for itself, was clearly palpable. It was really more about what Germany should be. The alternatives were prioritizing freedom or prioritizing unity. The Schumacher faction stood for the priority of unity. Germany must not bind itself to the West, but must remain unbound and open, for the sake of reunification. Adenauer favoured the principle of prioritizing freedom. There is unity, when we have freedom beforehand. That means we must bind ourselves to the West; only that way can the new start be successful. As an insult he was called the Chancellor of the Allies. Compared with Bismarck's Germany, this was now a completely new way of thinking, whereas the Schumacherian idea actually perpetuated Bismarck.

This is something, I believe, which to this day people are not sufficiently aware of. Here, Adenauer formed a new image of Germany, in which he clearly saw us bound up with the West. I was very much in favour of it. We had the feeling that Germany, after the breakdown of the Bismarckian ideal, must be redesigned as a German state, so with this approach we also stood at a new beginning. That included the idea that Christianity had a supporting role in this.

[6] The SPD is the *Sozialdemokratische Partei Deutschlands*, Social Democratic Party of Germany, founded in 1945.

Did you get to know Adenauer?

Not personally, no.

Were you always a very political person too?

I have never attempted to exert myself politically, but I always had a great personal interest in politics, and the philosophy that stands behind it. Because politics lives off a philosophy. Politics cannot simply be pragmatic, in the sense of 'we'll do something'. It must have a vision of the whole. That has always concerned me. There's also the fact that the nuncio [the ambassador of the Vatican to the Federal Republic] lived nearby then, Corrado Bafile.[7] The good nuncio came to me, the young professor, and offered me the use of his gardens, saying his gardens are my gardens, and read a presentation out to me. That was very moving, that a man who was at least an archbishop and of very high rank came to me in complete humility, with a cordial openness, to hear my opinion. Somehow the feeling of being in relationship to Rome was there, although this remained very loose.

The Der Spiegel *affair took place in your Bonn years, the first scandals about Franz Josef Strauß, then the struggles of the left against the Adenauer administration, the Cuba missile crisis . . . you were just thirty-two years old then.[8]*

---

[7] Corrado Bafile (4 July 1903 – 3 February 2005) was nuncio to the Federal Republic of Germany from 1960 to 1975. Cardinal Ratzinger conducted his funeral in St Peter's Basilica.

[8] The *Spiegel* Affair took place in 1962, when the German political magazine *Der Spiegel* alleged bribery of political officials was taking place in return for defence contracts. The magazine was accused of treason and its offices occupied by police. It led to legal changes establishing the freedom of the press, and is therefore considered an important turning point in the consolidation of democracy in the early years of the Federal Republic.

Such things were very significant to me, especially everything that was happening with Germany, as I've said. I am still a convinced Adenauerian. The fact that we are living in a long period of peace is largely thanks to Adenauer. Because giving precedence to unity would have probably meant that war would come at some point.

8

Vatican II: A Dream and a Trauma

Meeting Cardinal Joseph Frings is something included among the fateful encounters in your biography. Was that at a concert in Cologne Gürzenich, as is often reported, or at the lecture about the theology of the Council at Bensberg?

I wasn't with him at the concert, but I gave a lecture at the Catholic Academy in Bensberg about the theology of the Council, and Frings took part as a member of the audience. We went for a walk down the wide corridors and discussed things with one another. He was then bold enough to invite me to write the text for the Genoese Conference.

Frings was a member of the preparatory commission of the Council. He received all the draft texts, the so-called schemata, which he soon passed on to you, to critique and suggest improvements. What was your first impression of him?

We had already met before in Cologne. As a professor, one has an image of the competent bishop. He was a true native of the Rhineland, from Neuss; the slightly ironic, cheerful type of Rhinelander, and was noble and cordial with it. And it became clear with this first visit that we understood each other.

Later, each evening before your submission to the Council, Frings memorized what you had dictated to him on tape, in order then to present it freely at the meeting on the next day. He must have had an incredible ability to memorize texts. Was he already blind by the time of your first meeting?

Almost. He could still read in 1959, but with difficulty. You had to hold a table-lamp to the text for him.

The date is 19 November 1961, the day of the historic speech in Genoa.[1] Through this speech, the Council, whose course was being fixed by the specifications of the Curia, got a new orientation. Frings was invited to speak on the Council and the world of modern thought. He gave the speech, but it was your text. Did Frings provide you with set requirements?

No, he let me have complete freedom.

And you didn't consult with any others? Maybe a theologian of the Council, Jedin for example?

No, absolutely not. I had discretion because you're not allowed to discuss these things with others. But Frings by then could not read the speech himself. In Genoa he spoke the first sentence, then someone continued reading it.

As the author of such an important text, were you not very curious and excited about the reaction, about how it had come across?

Certainly, yes, yes. Indeed.

---

[1] Frings's speech was called 'Das Konzil auf dem Hintergrund der Zeitlage im Unterschied zum ersten vatikanischen Konzil' ('The council on the background of the present time in contrast to the First Vatican Council').

Whether one is perhaps even booed off the stage?

[Laughs] I don't remember now when I saw the cardinal. It was probably soon after. But I don't remember any of what he said to me then any more.

Presumably he thanked you. He did not conceal the fact that he was not the author.

He immediately informed humanity of that fact himself at that point. [Laughs]

Bishop Hubert Luthe, then Frings's secretary, who you knew from studying together in Munich, described to me how the famous meeting between the Cardinal and John XXIII came about. After the Genoa speech, he had to go to the preparation commission in Rome. There, one day he got a call. Papa Giovanni would like to speak to Cardinal Frings. 'I fetched the Cardinal around noon,' reports Luthe, 'he requested the cape and said "Mr Chaplain, put the red cloak around me once more, perhaps it is the last time."' The encounter with the Pope went completely differently than was feared anyway. 'Your eminence,' John XXIII said, 'I must thank you. I read your speech this evening, which has such a happy harmoniousness of thought.' Frings had given voice to everything that he meant for the Council, but was not able to express himself. Frings answered: 'Holy Father, I did not write any of the lecture, a young professor wrote it.' Then the Pope said: 'Mr Cardinal, I did not write my last encyclical myself. It comes down to a matter of where one identifies himself.' How did you hear about this scene?

Cardinal Frings told me about the meeting with Papa Giovanni himself; that he was called to see Papa

Giovanni and was then very uneasy. But otherwise I haven't really been told about how people reacted.

Did you have an encounter with John XXIII?

No. I came to the Council in October 1962; by then he was already seriously ill.

So far, the preparations for the Council were completed. You had looked through the schemata *and submitted your judgement. Do you remember the day of your departure to Rome?*

We went first to the bishops' graves in Cologne Cathedral, Cardinal Frings, Luthe and I. The cardinal then looked for a long time at the place where he would one day be buried. Only then did we go to the airport.

In Rome were all three of you housed in the historical German priests' college, the so-called Anima?

The cardinal and Luthe stayed in the Anima [the Collegio Teutonico di Santa Maria dell'Anima], as, incidentally, did all the Austrian bishops. There was no place left for me, so the Rector procured me a room at the Hotel Zanardelli, which was just around the corner. But from the celebration of the mass onwards, for breakfast, I was in the Anima, except during the siesta; that is something I learned then is certainly important in Rome. In the second period I stayed in the Palazzo Pamphili, which adjoins St Agnes in the Piazza Navona. I only stayed in the Anima for the third and fourth period.

How did you enjoy Roman life? The Piazza Navona for example?

It was all new to me. In the morning, children passed by in uniform on their way to school. They had no satchels, but carried their books in their hand, held together by a ribbon. I found that very amusing. The surroundings were very lively: there were vendors, the barber shop was full, the customers still all had shaving soap applied. Every day I did my walk and got to know the environment, sometimes with the cardinal. He was blind and had to be led. It once happened that I lost all sense of direction, and didn't know where to continue walking. It was an embarrassing situation. 'How would you describe this place in which we are standing?' he said. I described a statue that was standing there, of an Italian politician. 'Ah, that is Minghetti, then we must go on towards so-and-so.' The Roman life, this cheerfulness, the fact that a large portion of life plays itself out on the street and everything is rather noisy – I found this very amusing and interesting. In the Anima it was lovely to get to know so many people, the Austrian bishops, the young chaplain of the Anima. Cardinal Frings called cardinals to visit us from all over the place. Bishop Volk, a man with a great intellect and a great organizer, gathered together international groupings of bishops in his apartment in the Mater Dei villa; I was always there. It was here that I then also got to know Lubac.

Was it your first encounter with the French Jesuit and theologian, who had received a teaching ban from his order?

It was magnificent for me now to see him myself. He was very simple, very humble and very kind. It immediately felt as if we were old friends, despite there being a huge age gap between us, and a clear-cut difference in our achievements, the achievements of life. He was always very friendly and genuinely fraternal. Daniélou was also an amusing man [Jean Daniélou, French cardinal]. Lubac had certainly suffered then. He had taken a shot to the head during the First World War, and suffered terribly with headaches. But he never bore a grudge against the Germans.

Lubac had taken part in the French Resistance during the Second World War. How did you communicate? In French?

Français, oui.

During the period of the Council in Rome, did you sometimes stop for a couple of drinks with someone along the way? Did anyone say, come on, let's go and get a glass of wine, a drink of beer?

Not as a pair, no, but as part of a small group. Especially in the theological commission. Then we often drank plentifully in Trastevere.

Plentifully?

[The Pope laughs loudly]

Did you tell Henri de Lubac what he meant to you? What he had opened up for you, for example in his book Catholicisme *and his other works, with his new accentuation of the universal salvific significance of the Catholic Church and his co-founding of the* Nouvelle Théologie*?*

He actually didn't want to let you feel his greatness, somehow. He was very simple and unimaginably hard-working. I remember him falling very ill once in the theological commission. He was bedridden, but he had a book from the sixteenth century delivered to him from the city library, by an author on whom he wrote, and he lay in bed and worked.

He definitely bore a certain resemblance to—

No, I am not nearly so hard-working, I really must say. Congar [Yves Congar, French cardinal] was also incredibly hard-working. At the theological commission he never left his seat during the breaks, but would stay in his place and continue working.

Which theologians do you actually appreciate the most?

I would still say Lubac and Balthasar.

We are yet to speak about Hans Urs von Balthasar. What interested you about the setting of the Council in Rome?

At first, simply the universality of Catholics, the diverse polyphony, as people from all parts of the world encounter each other, as everybody is united in the same episcopate, can speak with each other, and find a way forward together. Then the encounters with great figures, to see Lubac once, even to speak with him, Daniélou, Congar, all the greats, that was extraordinarily exciting for me. Or to discuss things in the circle of bishops too. So the diverse polyphony and just encountering great people who were decision-makers, these were genuinely unforgettable experiences for me.

Were you also at the gatherings in St Peter's Basilica?

Yes, from the moment when I was an official conciliar theologian, but not before, of course.

You were with your brother in Rome for Easter in 1962, the first time in your life, and you lived with religious sisters in the vicinity of St Peter's. Why had you not made this journey earlier?

Because, I must say, a slight anti-Roman resentment had been imparted to us by our studies.

Not in the sense that we would have denied the primacy, denied obedience to the Pope, but that one had a certain inner reserve towards the theology that was done in Rome. In this sense there was a certain distance. I never went so far as a fellow student, however, who said: 'I would rather travel to Jerusalem than to Rome.' In any case one had no particular urge to go to Rome. Added to that we were weakly equipped financially, so it didn't come on the horizon as an option at all. The travel options available were not as good as today; it was a very long train ride.

How was it then the first time? Were you enthusiastic, fulfilled?

I was quite level-headed there. Of course I was thrilled with the ancient Christian sites, the catacombs, Saint Priscilla, Chiesa di San Paolo dentro le Mura, Saint Clement. The necropolis around St Peter as well, naturally. But not in the sense that I was floating on clouds, so to speak; rather because there the origins were within reach, the greatness of this continuity.

When you stood in St Peter's Square for the first time, did you put your arm round your brother's shoulders and say:

'Now we are here, in our home, dear Georg, in the centre of Christianity?'

Yes, but we Ratzingers are not quite so emotional. I mean, it was certainly impressive. The main thing, as I said, was the continuity with the origin, genuinely from Peter and the Apostles onwards. Around the Mamertine Prison, for example, where you can really trace things back to the time of the beginning. But the fascination expressed itself somewhat intellectually and inwardly, rather than us breaking out in cheers, so to speak.

Was this trip already a preparation for the Council?

There was certainly an enthusiasm within, that John XXIII had awakened. He fascinated me from the beginning onwards because of his total unconventionality. I liked that he was so direct, so simple, so human.

You were a follower of John XXIII?

I certainly was, yes.

A real fan?

A real fan, one can say.

When the Council was announced – do you remember now how you heard of it, and where you were?

Not exactly, no. I'm certain I heard about it on the radio. Then, of course, we spoke about it among the professors. It was a profound moment. The announcement of the Council had already provoked questions – How will it go? How can it all be carried out correctly? – but also great hopes.

Were you there from the first to the last day, in all four sittings?

Completely, yes. I was formally put on leave as a professor by the ministerial authorities in Germany.

You probably didn't see any of the sights of the city during the Council.

Very little time, one was very much made use of. Of course I took my walk every day, but that stayed within the vicinity of the Anima, where there is indeed much to be seen. The French national church, St Luigi, the Pantheon, St Eustace, the Sapienza and so forth, Palazzo Madama, but I could not see much otherwise.

The Council involved an unbelievable amount of work?

I don't want to exaggerate. So, it didn't break my back. But there was certainly lots to do, especially because of all the meetings.

Were you still able to get any sleep?

Yes, yes, that is non-negotiable for me. [Laughs] I'll never let that be infringed upon.

How did you actually communicate? You could only speak a little Italian.

A little, yes. Well, I functioned with it, somehow. I had reasonable Latin. Although I must say I had never studied theology in Latin, never spoke Latin like the Germanikers (German-speaking theology students that study at the Collegium Germanicum in Rome, founded in 1552 by Pope Julius III). We did everything in German. So for me to speak in Latin was something quite new. Therefore the possibilities for contributing that were at my disposal were limited. I could speak *Français* reasonably well, of course.

You hadn't yet gone on an Italian course?

No. [Laughs] I had no time, there was so much to do.

Did you take a dictionary with you?

Certainly, yes.

So you practised 'learning by doing'?

Precisely.

And which experience do you remember most fondly?

We travelled to Capri with the cardinal on All Saints' Day. We looked around Naples beforehand, the various churches and so on. To make the journey to Capri was very adventurous back then. We took a boat, which swayed from side to side in an alarming way. We all vomited, even the cardinal. I had always been able to master it until then. But then Capri was really lovely. It was a real sigh of relief.

Which camp did you belong to at that time: the progressives?

Yes, indeed, I would say so. At that time progressive did not mean that you were breaking out of the faith, but that you wanted to understand it better, and more accurately, how it lives from its origins. I was of the opinion then that that was what we all wanted. Famous progressives like Lubac, Daniélou etc. thought likewise. The change of mood was indeed already noticeable by the second year of the Council, but it only began to loom clearly with the passing of the years.

Recent research shows that your contribution on the part of Cardinal Frings was even greater than you have revealed yourself. We've already mentioned the Genoa Speech. In addition there was a first lecture for the German-speaking bishops in the Anima, just before the opening of the Council, a kind of briefing. In accordance with Frings's instructions, a plan was made to torpedo the election of ten Council commissioners on 13 October, to oust the favoured candidates the Roman Curia had put forward.

Well, that was on his own initiative. I haven't interfered with business, technical or political matters. That genuinely was his idea; he first had to get to know the people there at Council, in order for him to select committee members from his own ranks.

How did that actually come about? Frings was certainly not known to be a revolutionary.

No, absolutely not. He was known to be very conservative and strict. Everyone was surprised and astounded that he now took on a leading role. He even saw it that way himself; we spoke about it. He explained that, when exercising governance in the diocese, a bishop is responsible for the local church before the Pope and before the Lord. But it is something different if we are called to a Council to exercise shared governance with the Pope. A bishop then assumes his own responsibility, which no longer consists simply in obedience to the papal teaching office, but rather in asking what needs to be taught today, and how that teaching is to proceed. He was very aware of this. He distinguished between the normal situation of a Catholic bishop and the special situation of a Council Father, in which one is fully involved in shared decision-making.

Did he come to Rome with precise ideas ready?

I wouldn't say so, no. He had sent all the *schemata*, which I had by no means judged as negatively as they were judged subsequently. I sent him many corrections, but I had not laid hands on the substance of the whole, except in the case of the decree on revelation. That could have been improved. We agreed that the basic orientation was there, but on the other hand there was much to improve. Primarily, that it be less dominated by the current Magisterium, and had to give greater voice to the Scriptures and the Fathers.

You were awarded a leading role in the 'coup meeting' in the German priests' college, the Anima, on 15 October 1962. A new text, an alternative to the Roman draft edition, was brought to the table and then reproduced in 3,000 copies and distributed to the Council Fathers.

To call it a 'coup meeting' is too strong. But we were of the opinion that something different had to be said precisely about the theme of revelation, different from what was taking shape in that first edition. The draft still maintained a neo-scholastic style, and didn't take enough account of our findings. For me, 'revelation' was of course a predetermined topic, because of my post-doctoral work. So I'd already worked with it, but everything was contributed by invitation of his Eminence, and within his sights. Afterwards I was accused of deceiving the cardinal or some such. I really must repudiate that. We were both convinced in unison that we had to serve the cause of the faith and the Church. Also, in order to address this cause in a new terminology, in a new way, we wanted to clarify the proper relationship between Scripture, Tradition and the Magisterium, so that this relationship could really be understood and justified. That was then picked up.

How many people were involved at this meeting?

I can remember there was a discussion among cardinals only, and another with professors, but I cannot say exactly now.

It must have been dominated by an enormous tension.

No, actually we weren't really aware that we were doing anything stupendous. We didn't make any decisions there, but developed ideas. How it then got spread about the whole Council, I do not know. Of course we were awash with polemics: that we produced a typically freemasonic text and such things.

You were charged with that?

[Laughs] Yes, yes, although I really shouldn't be held in suspicion of being a freemason.

It was your arguments, it was your text, which Cardinal Frings presented to those assembled in the Council chamber erected in St Peter's Basilica on 14 November 1962, and brought everything to a tipping point. The original draft was on the table, and everyone had blocked it. Unrestrained dispute could now begin.

The question being put to the vote was very complicated. Those who wanted new things had to vote no. And those who wanted old things, had to vote yes. Anyway, it was a very close vote. Those who won were those who wanted to stay with the original *schema*. So from a legal perspective there was a very slight majority in favour of maintaining the first draft of the text. But then Papa Giovanni saw that the majority was too thin to be viable, and decided that the vote should be reopened.

It is said that there was thunderous applause for Cardinal Frings in the Council Chamber.

I wasn't inside then. I also don't believe it.

There was no phone booth in front of St Peter's, let alone mobile phones in those days. How did you learn of these things back then?

Well, after the Council sitting, the cardinal came over. I can't remember now if he told us about it himself. We were all very excited about what the Pope would do. And very happy that he said that even if a purely legal perspective would permit the first draft to stay in force, we would begin afresh.

Seven days later, on 21 November, the withdrawal of the schema on the 'Sources of Revelation' took place, a text you had heavily criticized. The text was, they wrote at the time, 'defined by the anti-modernist mentality'. It was said to have a tone which was 'frosty, almost shockingly so'.[2] You yourself saw this withdrawal as the real turning point of the Council.

[The Pope laughs] Now I'm surprised that I spoke in such an audacious manner back then. It is correct that this was a real turn, insofar as the submitted text was put to one side and there was a completely new beginning to the discussion.

How was it meeting Karl Rahner? You initially worked on a few texts together. He was much older than you, thirty years.

Just twenty-three years I believe; he was born in 1904 and I was in 1927.

Of course, you're right. Were things complicated with him?

I wouldn't say so. He was someone who consciously wanted to be responsive to young people, to young theologians. That then facilitates someone like me working with him. At that time we had a very good relationship. When we worked on that text, I soon noticed, however, that we belonged to two different worlds of thought. He had completely come out of scholasticism, which was a great advantage for him, because he could engage in the accustomed style of discussion more intensely thereby. While I came from just the Bible and the Fathers.

---

[2] In Joseph Ratzinger: *Die erste Sitzungsperiode des Zweiten Vatikanischen Konzils. Ein Rückblick*, Köln, J.P. Bachem Verlag, 1963. 'Vortrag an der Universität, Bonn vom 18. Januar 1963, ergänzt mit einem Vorwort', p. 38.

You already knew each other from previous encounters. How did your collaboration actually work in practice? Did you sit together at a desk in a room?

In 1962 we often worked as a pair in a room; at least, we worked on a text together. Later on, there wasn't this close collaboration.

You can work on a text in a team?

If you have a shared fundamental vision and intention, then yes.

You had already got to know Hans Küng at a dogmatics conference at Innsbruck in 1957. Did you meet at the Council?

Yes, mostly at the beginning, later less so. We sometimes had a cup of coffee in St Peter's Square, on the Via della Conciliazione. He didn't contribute to the commission's work in any case, but only talked privately to groups of bishops. So we did indeed meet often, but not in a working relationship.

Küng recognized early on that one can achieve a lot even if not a participant, by making oneself available for the media almost as an interpreter of the proceedings, and thereby standing more in the foreground than some others who are working hard on texts.

Yes, yes.

The Council had been announced on 25 January, and already by 1960 he had written a book with the title The Council and Reunion.[3] *Did he contribute something to the Council himself?*

---

[3] *The Council and Reunion* (London: Sheed and Ward, 1960).

He was certainly able to shape the opinions of bishops along the way, but he did not take part in working on texts.

Did you meet Cardinal Montini at the Council, the later Pope Paul VI?

I don't think so, no. I first met him as Archbishop of Munich.

You once criticized him heavily when he was Pope and you a professor in Regensburg, because he had not only suspended the use of the old Missal, but immediately forbade it.

'Heavily' is too strong, I think.

Apparently he did not resent you for it.

No.

Or maybe – he punished you by making you a bishop.

No, ha ha. No, he was safe in the knowledge that he and I were fundamentally in alignment.

The 1960s were a particularly colourful time. There was the Vietnam War, the hippie movement, Beatlemania, the sexual revolution. Did the Council Fathers perceive any of this at all?

I think these developments were indeed in the offing in the first half of the 1960s, but it was only in the second half that the dramas fully manifested. In any case, during the Council they weren't dominating the world scene yet. It all erupted in 1968.

Even so, by 1963 the play by Rolf Hochhuth, Der Stellvertreter, appeared, about Pope Pius XII and his behaviour towards the Nazis. The ensuing discussions ensured that the explosive power of this subject was made clear to the Catholic Church. However, instead of getting to grips with the Holocaust, fascism, the complicity of the Church, the Council debated the collective guilt of the Jews for the crucifixion of Christ. This omission still creates a negative image of the Church. Why was the importance of this debate not recognized by anyone at the Council?

Well, then it was not yet known that Pius XII had protected the Jews; one looked at this piece simply as a malicious distortion that didn't warrant any great attention. Golda Meir, Ben Gurion and many others had eagerly thanked Pius XII for his efforts. In the Jewish consciousness he was considered one of the great, light and positive forces at work. After Hochhuth this general perception only changed slowly at first, and then suddenly a new, completely different view of history was here; as if the Pope had been operating with the Nazis. That was just so absurd that one couldn't argue with it. In those years we had many encounters with Jews, and none of them expressed anything along those lines. Everyone was very insistent, however, that there had to be a declaration from the Council along the lines of defining the relationship between the Church and Judaism in positive terms. A declaration that offers a positive assessment of Judaism and dismantles the old prejudices, by means of which such a thing was able to happen.

This was very important. Here the Council arrived at a statement which to this day is acknowledged by

Jewish people as a pivotal document on this issue.[4] On the part of my Jewish friends, this issue has also never surfaced, so anyone who wants to push this case against Pius XII has to explain why it hasn't got very far in Jewish circles.

Putting Pius XII completely to one side — that the drama of the world war, of atheistic, totalitarian, dehumanizing political systems of the West and East, was not addressed seems completely incomprehensible from today's perspective.

The situation really was different then. There was this tremendous pressure from the Soviet Union, which had already swallowed up half of Europe. The Cuba missile crisis was seen as a signal that the world could explode at any moment. Everyone knew that Hitler was a criminal, and that Germany had done monstrous things at the hands of a criminal mob. But the present danger was so strong that you no longer reflected on the issues of the past, but saw everything under the weight of this present danger.

Your books about the individual sittings of the Council were your first prominent publications. They were even serialized in a daily newspaper.

Yes, it was good, but no great feat. Retrospectively, it was a minor account. The first was a lecture which I gave in a big auditorium in Bonn, which was completely packed. That was really an academic event. It was about information and interpretation, letting interested persons

---

[4] See *Nostra aetate*, the 'Declaration on the Relation of the Church with Non-Christian Religions of the Second Vatican Council', article 4.

know what actually happened at the Council. There was so much being said, this way and that, so there was a desire to hear the authentic voice of a participant, one jointly responsible in a way, and that was helpful.

There was no nasty heckling?

Good old Schmaus said I was a theological teenager and suchlike. But I didn't actually hear anything else from the German theological guild.

In your memoirs you speak of the 'excessive demands of the Council period'. Your health, as you took up your lectures in Tübingen in the summer semester, was in a 'rather bad condition'.[5]

That was the summer of 1966. Yes, well, it was a great strain. On the one hand I was still in Münster, but on the other I was already appointed in Tübingen. So I'm shuttling between Münster and Tübingen, which is no easy feat by train. Particularly in the early days, there was a lot to do in Tübingen, at such an exacting university with a very self-confident student body. On the other hand, the workload was also heavy in Münster. So I certainly had a great deal on.

In your memoirs you frequently mention the state of your health in passing. On your being appointed as the Bishop of Munich, you comment that it happened, 'although the poor condition of my health was generally known'.[6] So there were ongoing health problems?

[5] See *Milestones*, p. 136 (trans. altered).
[6] See *Milestones*, p. 153 (trans. altered).

[The Pope laughs] But one grows older and goes about things more carefully with it.

Have you ever had an operation?

No, I've just got a pacemaker, but there've been no other operations.

How long has it been since that was fitted?

I think it was 1997.

The Council had been going on for one year, when your mother died in December 1963, at your brother's house in Traunstein, after a long battle with cancer. Did you make it to her deathbed in time?

Yes, I left Rome prematurely and had already travelled home on All Saints' Day. She had just then become bedridden. If I remember correctly, I did not go back to Rome. I was able to accompany her through her last weeks anyway.

Did you know her end was close?

Yes. She had barely been able to eat since January. Since July she had only managed fluids. Nevertheless, she still ran the household. In October she collapsed while shopping in a grocery store. From then on it was clear, the end was close.

So you accompanied both your father, who had died already in August 1959, and your mother, in the last days of their lives.

That was very comforting for me. For all of us.

Your attitude towards the Council had gradually changed. In your book published in 1965, Ergebnisse und Probleme der 3. Konzilsperiode, *it states 'The Council, and the Church with it, is on the way. There is no reason for scepticism and resignation. We have every reason to have hope, good spirits, patience.' But by 18 June this same year, you declare before a Catholic student community in Münster that one is beginning 'to wonder, if things were not always better under the rule of the so-called conservatives, than they are able to be under the dominance of progressivism'. A year later, in 1966 at the Bamberg Katholikentag, you strike a balance which expresses scepticism and disillusionment. And with a lecture in Tübingen in 1967 you point out that the Christian faith is by now surrounded 'with a fog of uncertainty' as had 'hardly been seen before at any point in history'.[7] Is the new internal split, then beginning within the Church, and basically enduring to this day, to be considered as part of the tragic nature of the Council?*

I would say so, yes. The bishops wanted to renew the faith, to deepen it. However, other forces were working with increasing strength, particularly journalists, who interpreted many things in a completely new way. Eventually people asked, yes, if the bishops are able to change everything, why can't we all do that? The liturgy began to crumble, and slip into personal preferences. In this respect one could soon see that what was originally desired was being driven in a different direction. Since 1965 I have felt it to be a mission to make clear what we genuinely wanted and what we did not want.

Did you have pangs of conscience, as a participant, one who shares responsibility?

[7] *Introduction to Christianity*, p. 11.

One certainly asks oneself whether or not one did things rightly. Particularly when the whole thing unravelled, that was definitely a question one posed. Cardinal Frings later had intense pangs of conscience. But he always had an awareness that what we actually said and put forward was right, and also had to happen. We handled things correctly, even if we certainly did not correctly assess the political consequences and the actual repercussions. One thought too much of theological matters then, and did not reflect on how these things would come across.

Was it a mistake to convoke the Council at all?

No, it was right for sure. One can ask whether it was necessary or not, OK. And from the outset there were people who were against it. But in itself it was a moment in the Church when you were simply waiting on something new, on a renewal, a renewal of the whole. This was not to be something coming only from Rome, but a new encounter with the worldwide Church. In that respect the time was simply nigh.

The objective of the Council was, among other things, that a Pope, as you formulated it at the time, 'not only verifies texts from above, but rather helps to shape them from the inside'. A new physiognomy of the primacy was to make way for a new style of 'togetherness' between Pope and bishops, in turning back to 'that spirit of simplicity, which is the seal of their origin'. It seems connected, right here fifty years later, as you tried to implement your interpretation of the texts of the Council, in ecclesiastical office, in style, in word, in deed, including even the appearance of the Pope. Correct?

Absolutely, yes.

9

Professor and Bishop

In the summer of 1963 Joseph Ratzinger accepted a chair at the Catholic Faculty of the University of Münster, a city marked by its student culture. The young professor shared a one-storey residential building on the Annette-von-Droste-Hülshoff-Allee with his sister, and several students from Bavaria. They ate Sunday lunch together, sometimes in a restaurant in the immediate vicinity with the lovely name 'Gasthaus zum Himmelreich'.[1] His departure from Bonn was the consequence of an upset. On the one hand, some of his doctoral students from overseas were having problems with the faculty; on the other, there was envy and resentment towards the young theologian of the Council from influential fellow professors. 'You've driven him out', intimated Hubert Jedin. Ratzinger himself saw the change as something that 'suggests to me the hand of providence', even if this phrase initially referred to two of his doctoral students, for whom he now hoped for better conditions. In Münster his Advent sermons in the cathedral soon aroused attention from the public. In discussion meetings, with Johann Baptist Metz and Hans Urs von Balthasar, for example, he showed himself to be a moderator who could untangle complicated things and clarify the different positions.

[1] Translated literally, 'Kingdom of Heaven guesthouse'.

Holy Father, was the departure from Bonn one of those solitary decisions, that one sort of encounters in the night, sometimes arising from annoyance?

No. I had of course discussed the matter with Cardinal Frings, since I was his Council adviser as a professor of the faculty at Bonn, and could automatically assume that I could continue to discharge this function if I accepted the call to Münster. The cardinal said to me, in a paternal way, with great human kindness, and coming from rich life experience, that I could accept the call to Münster if my preferred discipline was really dogmatics and not fundamental theology. On the basis of that positive reason I eventually accepted the call to Münster.

In Münster you ran into a circle of philosophers gathered around the philosopher Josef Pieper (1904–77). You met every Saturday at 3 p.m. in Pieper's house at 10 Malmedyweg. Was that a kind of gentleman's club?

[Laughs] Yes, he met every Saturday afternoon with Bishop Volk, with Lausburg, the Romantic scholar, and Beckmann, the Latinist; then I also joined the club. We had good conversations, in which he primarily related his travels, his reflections. It was a lovely balance of specialists in different disciplines based at one university.

How was this circle orientated? As a sort of conservative fraternity?

Absolutely not. Pieper was then understood as a progressive, just as I was. As someone who was on the way to new things, as with his fresh interpretation of Thomas Aquinas. He fascinated those who heard his lectures. What

Guardini was for Munich, Pieper was for Münster. Only later did he go in the same direction as I did, and Lubac. We saw that the very thing that we want, something new, is being destroyed. Then he energetically opposed it.

Hans Urs von Balthasar, the great Swiss theologian. When did you actually meet him?

I'd already read him as a student of course. In 1949 I was at a lecture he gave at the University of Munich. In Freising I was already utilizing some ideas of his in my lectures. I only met him personally in Bonn in 1960. The book by Alfons Auer, *Weltoffener Christ*, had just been published. Balthasar took the position that this sort of openness to the world was fatal, and invited Alfons Auer, Gustav Siewerth, me, and few others, to speak about it in Bonn. Why he invited me, I do not know. Auer then didn't come, so the aim of the conversation was not fulfilled.

But from then on a friendship developed? He is a very different sort of person to you, in any case.

He was a real aristocrat, tall, slender, noble, aristocratically reserved. We simply understood each other very well, from the first moment on.

You continually say 'I am no mystic', but now you befriend a mystic.

Yes, why not?

You were already in Münster by 1965, when Balthasar was given an honorary doctorate. An extensive exchange of letters followed, and in the 1980s frequent telephone calls. What was it like, speaking on the phone with him?

Ha ha, completely normal! 'Here isch Balthasar', he always said, so real Swiss German, Yes, and then we spoke completely normally with each other on the telephone.

Did you call him Urs?

No, no, we weren't on first-name terms.

You gave lectures together at the Catholic Academy in Munich, and published a book about Mary together. Your book Dogma and Preaching *is dedicated to Balthasar.*[2] *In turn he dedicated his five-volume* Explorations in Theology *to you. What makes this intense relationship special?*

I came across him properly in 1961 when *Hochland* sent me two of his recently published volumes of essays to review, *Verbum Caro* and *Sponsa Verbi*. In order to review them, of course, I had to read them thoroughly. From then on, Balthasar became a household word for me. Here, the theology of the Fathers was present, a spiritual vision of theology, which is genuinely developed out of faith and contemplation, which goes down to the depths and is new at the same time too. Thus it wasn't just academic stuff, with which one ultimately can do nothing, but a synthesis of erudition, genuine professionalism and spiritual depth. That was what enraptured me. From then on we were connected to each other.

Real kindred spirits?

[2] Joseph Ratzinger, *Dogma and Preaching*, Chicago: Franciscan Herald Press, 1985 [1973].

Certainly. Even if I can't keep up with his erudition. But the inward intention, the vision as such, was shared.

You couldn't keep up with his erudition?

No, absolutely not. Really. It is unbelievable what this person has written and done. He had no theology PhD. He was a scholar of German literature, and always said, when one wanted to select him to vote for anything in the theological commission: 'I'm no theologian, I can't do that!' and then he would say: 'We don't have a library in Basel.'

Did the relationship with Balthasar have a personal dimension, or was it only intellectual and spiritual?

That was certainly there too. For example, he once invited me to the Rigi.[3] A house that belonged to some rich person, and was put at his disposal. We were together for a few days on one of the Alps. When he went to mass, he always had a bundle of letters with him, which he threw into the letterbox. He had already written them early in the morning, in quantities, in his beautiful handwriting. Everything just flowed out of him that way. He also simply wrote the books down like this. The woman Capol, the secretary, then looked through them, corrected any possible mistakes, and prepare them for press.

How should one imagine the two of you on the mountain during those days?

---

[3] Von Balthasar founded a group called the Community of St John, based in a house in Rigi-Kaltbad.

[Laughs] Well, during the day we worked separately, we ate lunch together, then went for a walk. There you can hike in any case, without having to be a mountaineer.

Did you also know Adrienne von Speyr, his spiritual companion? She was a doctor and a mystic, and Protestant originally. She dictated her visions, of the apocalypse for example, to Balthasar, who worked on them for publication.

No, she was no longer alive. In the years of the Council I couldn't stay in contact with him. That only came in the Tübingen years, and then she was already dead.

Was her work not so appealing to you?

Not to me, no. That differentiated us. One has to say he was someone defined by mysticism.

Did Balthasar criticize you? There is allegedly a statement of his which says: 'If Ratzinger does not continue to develop, he will lack an entire dimension.' It is about bearing the cross as your guiding star.

Oh really? Where is that?

I think your one-time colleague Johann Baptist Metz told me.

Ah, interesting. You spoke with Metz?

Yes.

And was it good?

I found it remarkable that at the end of his life he asks himself whether the concept of political theology, which he coined, was not a mistake, whether perhaps it's ultimately just been chaff. He meant something different from what was then understood by this term. Apparently he also regrets that you had interpreted his work as if it were almost a theology in the sense of Ernst Bloch's.

That was the case too, a little. He did something naïve. I was surprised, moreover, that he developed this very political theology as something new, apparently unaware that in 1935 Erik Peterson had already published an article, which grew from a dispute with Carl Schmitt about his idea of political theology, and fatally criticized it. But I have to add that Metz was repeatedly effective as a great stimulator of theological thinking, and certainly viewed the essential issues correctly.

Back to Balthasar and his having criticized you . . .

That's quite possible. He was a man with a comprehensive vision, and everyone can occasionally see things that other people don't. I find that completely normal.

From Münster you participated further in the Council, your lectures were packed, handwritten notes were copied out a hundredfold and circulated all over Germany. But after just three years, another farewell came, and not in the direction of Tübingen, where Hans Küng made a strong case for appointing you. Leaving places seems somehow to be a recurring feature of your life. And again, for friends, colleagues, observers, the departure was completely incomprehensible. Or are there reasons which you have not disclosed?

149

[Laughs] No. That really was a difficult decision for me. One reason for the departure was simply that Münster struck me as being too far north. I am such a proud Bavarian that to live in Münster long term was simply too far away from home. All the more so knowing my brother was living in Regensburg, I always wanted to go there [Georg Ratzinger had meanwhile been appointed as director of music at Regensburg Cathedral and director of the world-famous boys' choir, the Regensburger Domspatzen]. By train it was an endless journey. The other reason was that I had the feeling that with Johann Baptist Metz's political theology a new direction was emerging, which brings faith into politics in the wrong way.

How were you able to come to the conclusion that the conditions in Tübingen would actually be any different? In a Protestant city, where the Protestant professors would not necessarily fulfil your every wish. Just as you were becoming someone who had begun to criticize the Council.

I have to wonder at my naivety myself. Although I did have very good relations with many professors at the Protestant theology faculty. There were really outstanding people there: Otto Michel, Ulrich Wickert and so on. Martin Hengel was not yet there. Well, I had made the naïve assessment that Küng had a big mouth and said impudent things, but fundamentally wanted to be a Catholic theologian. He gave a really nice lecture about the unity of Scripture, which was genuinely very positive, and other things. I had not foreseen that he would then go on to break ranks repeatedly.

Tübingen (1966–9)

You moved from Münster to Tübingen in an old Opel car belonging to Vinzenz Pfnür, whom you called your 'Urschüler'. Why did you never get a driving licence?

I don't know . . .

Because your sister was so anxious?

No, no, I would never let myself be deterred. My father had said that all three children must get their licence. No one had done that for him. I simply had no time. And then, yes, I must say that I had the feeling I would run into trouble with such a machine. To steer a car back and forth across the world seemed too dangerous to me. There is some confusion about the Opel Kadett anyway. I got an assistant, Lehmann-Dronke, to drive me from Tübingen to Regensburg in an ancient VW Beetle, which had been inspected by a policeman who was suspicious of its archaic condition, but everything was in order. But I travelled from Münster to Tübingen by train.

You liked Tübingen immediately. You speak of the 'magic of the small Swabian town' for which you had 'very strong' feelings.[4]

Well, it is simply beautiful. Just the marketplace with its Protestant church, then the 'Gôgei' [the old vine-grower's district in the Old City], the meadows down by the Neckar and so on. From my house I could look up at the Wurmling Chapel, which was directly opposite.

---

[4] *Milestones*, p. 136.

Your students in Tübingen describe you as particularly person-able, although you never said too much.

I didn't know that. [Laughs] But I'm not such a chatty person in myself. My brother is completely different there.

Right from the start, it seems that your approach is always to work with whichever people are available. Your circle of students was therefore not homogeneous, because no one was excluded.

It's always a good thing to have diverse characters.

Your colloquia for doctoral students always began with Holy Mass, which was considered very exotic in Tübingen. Once, you visited Karl Barth in Switzerland, together with your students. How did this relationship come about?

Already from Gottlieb Söhngen onwards I was a sort of Barthian, if also critical. He was one of the fathers of theology with whom I had grown up. Then the connection with Balthasar came along; he was a great friend of Barth. And so we went there once. He was already an old man. We didn't have any deep conversations with him, but to meet him was certainly a beautiful thing.

Did you revere him a lot?

Yes, and he liked me too. During my Germany trip in 2010 President Schneider told me that Karl Barth always said to him: 'Read Ratzinger!'

Had you read Sartre yourself by then?

Sartre was someone you had to read. He wrote his philosophy mainly in cafés. Therefore it is less deep, but more penetrating, more realistic. He translated Heidegger's existentialism into concrete terms. Then one can see the alternatives much more clearly. Pieper worked that out very well.

Did you have any contact with Ernst Bloch in Tübingen?

I was once invited to Bloch's house. It was a small party, so maybe six or seven people. That was odd, I must say. There was an Arab there, perhaps it was even me who brought him along. Anyway, someone there had a hookah, and Bloch said: 'I've been wanting to have a go with one of these again for ages.' But then he showed that he couldn't handle it. [Laughs]

How did it come about that you had the honour of this invitation?

I can't remember any more, I couldn't say now.

Did your sister find interacting with professors difficult?

Well, such very strange types of people were not really her thing. But some individuals, Küng and others, we invited over often. She liked that a lot.

She was more reserved?

Yes, yes, very much so.

Was that a problem for you?

No.

She was not necessarily a socialite.

She certainly was not, no. But neither did she need to be.

In Tübingen you purchase your first television. Your brother Georg says it was because of your 'news addiction'.

[Short burst of laughter] No, I actually didn't want it at all, but I was very friendly with the student pastor, Starz, a very good man. He came to me one day and said: 'Hey you, today we're driving here and there and buying a television.' We actually got it in a supermarket. You could buy sausages and meat, and a few televisions were standing there between the tins of meat and the cans. We bought one, but it wasn't very good.

In 1968, your Introduction to Christianity *was published. The peculiar thing is that it was not actually intended as a book at first, was it?*

Yes. In Bonn the boss of the publishers Kösel, Dr Will, said that I should write a book about the essence of Christianity. He always came back to it, and was pushing me more and more strongly. In Tübingen, Küng and I took turns in our lectures. One semester I had the main course, he the next, so I had some free time. With such a free semester I thought that now the moment has come, now I've given this material as a lecture, it should become a book.

So Introduction to Christianity *did not originate with notes written by students?*

No, I drafted it in shorthand, then dictated it aloud and worked through it after that.

The work has been a classic for a long time, and has been published worldwide in countless editions. It has impressed generations of readers, not least Karol Wojtyla, later to be John Paul II. Were you surprised at its success?

Indeed, yes.

No one saw it coming?

No, not at all. It's still selling even today.

And it will continue to do so for many decades to come. You write in your own personal shorthand, with your own abbreviations. Someone said that one side of A4 is enough for you write a long lecture. Did you write the Jesus book in shorthand too?

Everything. Otherwise I would need too much time to write. This brings Rahner to mind, it was how we wrote then. He said once with a sigh: 'Well, it takes too much time to finish the thing.' [Laughs] It is much better when you write in shorthand.

The Swiss theologian Hans Küng has persecuted you over the course of decades with abuse and downright slander, like saying you were a nasty power-seeker, that you set up a surveillance system like the Stasi's, and even that you are still governing after your resignation as the 'shadow pope'. Yet, in 1968 you were still on the very best of terms. However, he had a completely different lifestyle to you. While your colleague drove up to the university in his Alfa Romeo, you still always arrived at work on an old bicycle. Compared with you he's almost like a Grand Burgher.

Of course he had completely different origins, from Sursee; they had a shoe shop, a noble burgher's house.

He was without doubt cut from a very different cloth to me.

One of your sayings was: 'I concur with my colleague Küng.' Küng expressed it vice versa: 'I am fundamentally of one opinion with my colleague Ratzinger.' You were both editors of a series of books, in which Küng's work The Church *was published.*[5]

That was the point where I clearly felt that things could not continue like this, and where I then withdrew from this editorship. That book was still edited by me, but I think it is the last one.

To whom did you explain this resignation?

I wrote a letter saying I no longer wanted to be co-editor.

You wrote it to Küng?

Maybe to Herder. I can't remember now.

Without an explanation?

That wasn't needed.

Küng must have judged that to be an affront.

We never quarrelled, but we saw – perhaps I saw it more than him – that things were diverging.

In the highly charged atmosphere of that '68-ers' time, the encyclical Humanae vitae *came along on 25 July, the so-called 'pill-encyclical' of Paul VI. How did you find that time?*

---

[5] *The Church* (London: Burns and Oates, 1967).

In the situation I was then in, and in the context of theological thinking in which I stood, *Humanae vitae* was a difficult text for me. It was certainly clear that what it said was essentially valid, but the reasoning, for us at that time, and for me too, was not satisfactory. I was looking out for a comprehensive anthropological viewpoint. In fact, it was John Paul II who was to complement the natural-law viewpoint of the encyclical with a personalistic vision.

In the ongoing course of your life Hans Küng emerged, as mentioned, as a powerful opponent. It is not like with Mozart and his counterpart Salieri, but you mostly have your former colleague to thank for your negative reputation, which still clung to you even after your election in 2005. What lay behind this?

Well, his theological path just went someplace else, and he got increasingly radical. I could not join in with this, I wasn't permitted to. Why I was then identified by him as an enemy, I do not know. Because others have written against him too, from Rahner onwards.

The hostilities are still sustained against you, up to the last.

That is something one has to accept.

You worked together with Karl Rahner at the Council, Hans Küng recommended you for the professorial chair at Tübingen; furthermore, you pronounced the left-winger Metz as your successor in Münster. Did you choose another side at some point? What happened?

I saw that theology was not the interpretation of the faith of the Catholic Church any more, but was devising how it could be and should be, on its own merits. For me that theology was incompatible with being a Catholic theologian.

In this period there was a petition for the abolition of celibacy that you co-signed. Was that a slip-up?

What Rahner and Lehman had devised was discussed in the Doctrinal Commission of the German Bishops' Conference, in which we were together. It was so complexly tangled, as things with Rahner just are. On one side there was a defence of celibacy, and on the other side an attempt to keep the question open and think further. I signed more out of friendship with the others. Of course that was not so fortunate. But I would say it was not a demand for the abolition of celibacy, it was a typically intricate Rahnerian yes-and-no text, so one could interpret it as being for one side or for the other.

You've always stressed that, on your part, there was no U-turn from your earlier ways of thinking.

I believe that anyone who reads what I have written can confirm that.

The crucial phase of the student rebellions subsequently began, with sit-ins, blockaded lectures, strikes. Did you witness the demonstrations on the street close up?

No.

With your youthful appearance you would probably have been able to pass yourself off as a student.

That might well be. [Laughs] At that time I was closely connected to the dean of the law faculty, Peters, whose office was near me. By the way, at this time I also joined this organization for the freedom of intellectual inquiry, Hans Maier obtained membership for me.[6] We worked closely with colleagues who wanted to call a halt to the crudest nonsense.

Was the student rebellion really a trauma for you, as Hans Küng never tired of spreading about?

Absolutely not. I never even had any disturbances in my lectures. Nonetheless, I dramatically experienced what terror there was then.

Hans Küng has linked his polemical work Infallible? *(from 1970), with the publication of* Humanae vitae. *Was it clear from this point, when you disputed that your colleague was still moving in the sphere of catholicity in your review of this book, that ties were finally cut?*

Yes, clearly.

To what extent did you contribute to Küng's ecclesiastical licence to teach being revoked in 1979?

I didn't directly contribute to that at all. In previous years I had occasionally been asked to give an opinion, but I always said: let him be. It had to be made clear that he was not theologically correct, but I never advised that measures be taken against

---

[6] The *Bund Freiheit der Wissenschaft* (BFW), 'Organisation for the Freedom of Science', founded in 1970 to oppose the student rebellions.

him. Cardinal Franjo Šeper, my predecessor at the Congregation for the Faith, was utterly outraged, as nothing had happened. He was really wound up. 'I have been here for fifteen years,' he said, 'the Church is being destroyed and we are doing nothing. If that happens once more, then I will stop it.' He had reached the point where he could no longer tolerate it, and could not reconcile his conscience with the fact that nothing had happened. John Paul II then invited the German cardinals – Höffner, Volk, me – as well as the Archbishop of Freiburg, and the Bishop of Rottenburg-Stuttgart, to speak about the matter with him. That was at Christmas-time. But the decision was already made. And we said, notwithstanding the abstention of the Bishop of Rottenburg, that it is not allowed to be changed, it must stand.

Was Küng judged, as he says, without the authorities listening to his side, or granting access to his file?

No. I was not yet even in Rome then, but there are procedures which would have been adhered to. The records of a case as such are not usually delivered, but he certainly knew how these things proceeded; he was questioned and could provide answers.

Regensburg (1969–77)

Finally, all should be well. The young professor is back in his beloved Bavarian homeland, which especially pleases his sister Maria and his brother Georg. Ratzinger is regularly elected as dean of the Catholic Faculty, and in 1976 is elected as Vice-Rector of the university. And he dreams of developing his theological oeuvre. Important works are published during this time, like *Das Geheimnis von Tod und Auferstehung* and *Das neue Volk Gottes. Entwürfe zur Ekklesiologie,* in which Ratzinger discusses 'the collegiality of the bishops' and 'the renewal of the Church', among other things. He is now especially able to tackle questions about death and immortality, eternal life, the Second Coming and the Last Judgement. He denotes the work devoted to these themes, *Eschatology,* as his most thorough book.

You don't remain anywhere long. Like a solitary perhaps, who doesn't necessarily adapt himself. You have departed from Bonn, from Münster, now from Tübingen.

I was Prefect from 1982 to 2005, after all.

But you wanted to stop after the first period.

OK, but it was clear that that wasn't going to happen. [Laughs]

In Regensburg, where you wanted to stay, you were not allowed to. Would that be the story of your life?

You can say so, yes.

You had set yourself up in Regensburg, built a house for yourself and your sister, but then you were abruptly torn away. You were shocked when the nuncio personally brought you the news that the Pope wanted to appoint you the new Bishop of Munich. Shock and incomprehension not only because you would no longer be teaching any theology, which you saw as your profession, but on account of, as you put it later, 'my unfamiliarity with the tasks of management and administration':[7] things one had to

*know in senior office. Was this the big rupture in your life,
the end of your dreams?*

Yes, but I also knew that you can't live on your dreams.

*After a night of wrestling with it, you signed the declaration of
consent in a hotel in Regensburg. What hotel was that?*

That was – my God, what's it called? When you come
from the train station into the city . . . anyway, it was
on the right-hand side, I don't know whether or not it
still exists.

*You had sought counsel from your confessor on this dramatic
night, Professor Johann Auer, a man you describe in your
memoirs as someone 'who had a very realistic knowledge of
my limitations, both theological and human'.*[8] *What did you
mean by 'human limitations'?*

Well, he was of the opinion – hmm, how should I put
it? – that I still had a lot to learn, that I was by no
means perfect, that I had problems. We were friends,
but he had expressed fraternal rebukes, just as a friend,
precisely because, yes, he saw my limitations.

But he actually encouraged you to take this step.

That was the funny thing. I had expected him to say:
'No, you can't do that!' Because otherwise he always
said: 'That's not for you!', or that I did such-and-such
wrongly, and so on. So I thought he'd say: 'That's not
for you.'

[7] *Milestones*, p. 151.
[8] *Milestones*, p. 152.

Was it possibly your shyness that was meant by 'human limitations'?

Perhaps not. But then again . . .

Your reserved manner, a former assistant said, went so deep that it required great skill to call you out from your glass cage.

[Laughs] That is a little excessive.

Anyway, with Auer you had someone with whom you could obviously speak about very personal matters.

Yes, yes.

München (1977–82)

After almost twenty-five years of teaching activities in German universities, Dr Joseph Ratzinger was named as the new Archbishop of Munich and Freising by Paul VI on 25 March 1977. In the Bavarian capital he came to be known as one of the most eloquent analysts of society, one who provided an evident contribution to the ethical issues of the day. There was high demand for his sermons. The following books appeared: *God is Near Us: The Eucharist, the Heart of Life, Christian Faith and Europe,* and *Faith, Renewal, Hope,* subtitled: *Theological Contemplations on the Present Situation of the Church.*[9]

---

[9] *God is Near Us: The Eucharist, the Heart of Life,* Augsburg: Sankt Ulrich, 2001. *Eucharistie – Mitte der Kirche,* München: Wewel, 1978; *Glaube – Erneuerung – Hoffnung. Theologisches Nachdenken über die heutige Situation der Kirche,* ed. Willi Kraning (*Faith, Renewal, Hope: Theological Contemplations on the Present Situation of the Church*), Leipzig: Sankt-Benno-Verlag, 1981.

On 6 August 1978, Paul VI died. At the subsequent conclave, after a rather volatile meeting of the Synod a year before, one of the first personal encounters with Karol Wojtyla, the Cardinal of Krakow, occurred. How do you remember this encounter?

Like this: he had already spoken occasionally in the conclave, and what he said really impressed me. I had the impression that he was a thoughtful person, with a significant philosophical formation, and a particularly pious, faithful, warm-hearted and kind person with it. All this was then confirmed by meeting face to face. This was a cultivated person who had humour, an affectionate humanity, and faith.

How did you communicate?

In German. He spoke very good German. It was his first and his best foreign language, which he learned from the first year of school.

Karol Wojtyla, first auxiliary bishop, then Archbishop of Krakow, was a participant in the Council, like you. You didn't run into him while in Rome?

Not at the Council. But I had already heard of him. I knew he was a philosopher, because he had just spoken at the philosophy congress in Naples.

Albino Luciano emerged from the conclave in August as John Paul I; he was soon named as the 'smiling Pope'. But just thirty-three days later the Catholic Church had to carry a Pope to the grave again. The great gathering of the Church had another sitting. As Cardinal of Munich you partici-pated in both conclaves. Something sensational was about to happen. With Karol Wojtyla, for the first time in 500 years, a non-Italian had been chosen to be Pope. Did you play a big part in his being elected?

No, I don't believe so. I was one of the youngest cardinals, and I also didn't want to presume that I would somehow play a role. I am fundamentally averse to plotting and suchlike, especially in the election of the Pope. Everyone should vote according to his conscience. OK, we German-speakers did speak with other, but without any conspiracies.

But they say it was the German-speakers around Cardinal König of Vienna who had given the choice of Karol Wojtyla considerable support.

Support, definitely, yes.

You completely restrained yourself?

I can only say that König spoke to various cardinals outside the conclave. What went on inside stays secret. As a very newly minted archbishop, I gave any public activities a wide berth. We German-speaking cardinals met, to give each other counsel on things. But I myself didn't engage in any kind of politics. That did not seem to be appropriate for someone in my situation.

Were you startled that it was the Pole?

No. Absolutely not. I was for him. Cardinal König had spoken to me. And my own personal, albeit brief, acquaintance with him had convinced me that he was the right man.

On 16 October the 264th pontificate of the Roman Catholic Church began. The new man, who introduced himself as someone 'from a distant land', heralded an era in which the world was to change in ways that no one thought possible. Through the choice of Wojtyla, a new situation had emerged for you. Because now someone had become Pope who absolutely wanted to have you, and moreover, in Rome.

Something I didn't yet know then, but that would soon be revealed.

How soon was that? When exactly did the call first come?

I can't put a date on it now. I knew that he wanted to have me on board. A year earlier there, the post of Prefect at the Congregation for Catholic Education was vacant. He already wanted me then. I said: 'It won't work. I've been in Munich such a short time, I've made a vow, I can't just go now.' Then it went to Cardinal Baum from Washington. After that, I couldn't really say no again. That is, I still had one condition, which I thought couldn't be met. I said: 'I can only accept it if I am allowed to continue publishing.' He was unsure at first, but he looked into it and established that Cardinal Garrone, who was the incumbent before Baum, had published. He then said: 'You can.'

Isn't it an affront to a Pope to have conditions?

[Laughs] Maybe, but I deemed it my duty to say that, because I felt an inward obligation to be able to say something to humanity.

Prefect (Rome, 1982–2005)

With the farewell to Munich it becomes clear how anchored Ratzinger was in this city, in Bavaria as a whole. The office of bishop had been occupied by a shepherd who was in touch with the people. Never before had a German cardinal departed with so much praise, with such great sorrow from society at large, which even included a live broadcast on ARD.[1] There was certainly a dark sense of foreboding. Ratzinger knew that the news which would soon come as a result of his activities in Rome, and bearing his signature, would not only include positive things. And so it was that the celebrated young former Archbishop of Munich, who was met with such grief on his departure, soon became the 'Pope's guard dog'.

Holy Father, on 25 November 1981 you were appointed Prefect of the Congregation for the Doctrine of the Faith, and hence alongside the Pope as the supreme guardian of the faith of the Catholic Church. On 1 March 1982 you reported for duty in Rome. It is said that the first major meetings you held in office were conducted in Latin.

---

[1] Arbeitsgemeinschaft der öffentlich-rechtlichen Rundfunkanstalten der Bundesrepublik Deutschland.

I couldn't yet speak Italian. I'd only learned to join in conversations. Of course that remained my handicap too. I wasn't able to steer matters when speaking Italian then, so did it in Latin.

In the hope that you would be understood.

Then everyone could really still speak Latin, that wasn't a problem.

How was your first encounter with John Paul II in the Vatican? Was there a conversation about the fundamental orientation of the pontificate, and about your tasks particularly?

No. I did have the weekly audience. That gave plenty of time to interact. We didn't undertake any deliberations on policy. It was actually quite clear what a prefect had to do.

You once said that you got to know this great man better by concelebrating the Holy Mass with him than by analysing his books. Why was that?

Yes, well, if you concelebrated with him, you felt the inward proximity to the Lord, the depth of faith which he would then plunge into, and you really experienced him as a man who believes, who prays, and who is indeed marked by the Spirit. This was more the case than if you read his books, although they also gave an image of him, but they certainly didn't let the whole of his personality energe.

You had very different temperaments. Why did things work so well between you both? Or maybe that is precisely why it worked so well?

Maybe that's why, yes. He was a man who needed companionship, needed life, activity, needed encounters. I, however, needed silence more, and so on. But precisely because we were very different, we complemented each other well.

And simply because you liked each other?

Yes.

Because the chemistry was right?

That is correct.

And the same faith was there?

Exactly.

That makes it nice and easy.

Sure. Because you always know that you want the same thing.

Was there private contact too? Outings, meals, walks together?

Meals certainly, but always with a little group. No walks, actually.

And above all, no skiing.

[Laughs] No, I can't, unfortunately.

Did you use 'Du' when speaking with one another?[2]

---

[2] 'Du' is the German word for 'you', used between friends and family members, as opposed to 'Sie', a polite term used in more formal settings.

No.

As Archbishop of Munich, or as Prefect in Rome, were you assigned by the Pope to do any tasks in Poland? Tasks to support the opposition movement Solidarność?

No I wasn't.

You went to Poland several times in this period.

Certainly, yes, but not so that . . . There was a direct relationship then.

The state security service of the GDR had you under observation. There is a file on you.

Indeed, yes, but there was nothing to find.

Were you actively involved in the Pope's Ostpolitik?

We spoke about it. It was clear that Casaroli's politics [Cardinal Agostino Casaroli is regarded as the architect of the Vatican's *Ostpolitik* under John Paul II and Paul VI; under Karol Wojtyla he served as Cardinal Secretary of State from 1979 to 1990], although well intentioned, had basically failed. The new approach from John Paul II came from his own life experience, from contacts with these powers and forces. Of course, one could not hope then that this regime would soon collapse. But it was clear that, rather than trying to be reconciled with it through conciliatory compromises, one must strongly confront it. That was John Paul II's basic insight, which I shared.

There were also disputes with one another.

No.

But probably differences. The Pope's prayer meeting in Assisi with representatives of the world religions, for example; that just wouldn't have been your favourite idea.

That's right, certainly. But we didn't argue about it, because I knew that he wanted the right thing, and, vice versa, he knew that I took a slightly different line. He said to me before the second meeting in Assisi that it would be very nice for him if I came along, so then I went too. It was also structured better then, because the objections I had were taken on board. It was then structured in a way that meant I could gladly participate.

It is alleged that John Paul II had a saying he used when confronted with a complicated question: 'What will Cardinal Ratzinger say about it?' I asked you at the start of our first book, Salt of the Earth, *'Is the Pope afraid of you?'*[3]

No. [Vigorous laughter] But he took our stand very seriously. I can tell you a little anecdote here. Pius XII was once asked by a nuncio whether or not he was allowed to do such-and-such with a certain problem, even if it was not entirely in keeping with the rules. The Pope mulled it over and then said: 'You can. If, however, the Holy Office discover it, I cannot protect you.' [Laughs]

One of your most sensational publications as Prefect was the declaration Dominus Jesus. *It is about the uniqueness of the Catholic Church, which unleashed fierce criticism. Whether*

---

[3] *Salt of the Earth*, p. 9.

or not you wrote this document yourself is a question being puzzled over to this day.

I deliberately never wrote any of the documents of the office myself, so that my opinion does not surface; otherwise I would be attempting to disseminate and enforce my own private theology. Such a document should be grown organically, from the soil of the relevant offices responsible. Of course I was a co-worker, and did some critical redrafting etc. But I didn't write any documents myself, including *Dominus Jesus*.

At the time the impression was conveyed that even the Pope was against this document.

Which is not true. He called me one day and said: 'I want to speak about it during the *Angelus* and make it quite clear that I am in complete agreement with it, so I'm asking if you will write the text for the *Angelus* yourself, so there can be no doubt that the Pope is at one with you.' So I wrote a text. But then I thought I shouldn't write so starkly, it didn't fit. The content was clear, but I made the style more elevated. He then said to me: 'Is it really waterproof? Are you sure?' – 'Yes, yes.' But the opposite was the case. Because of this more elevated style everyone said: 'Ah, even the Pope has distanced himself from the cardinal.'

How was it with the great confession of guilt in 2000, whereby the Catholic Church apologized for her past failings and offences? Did you oppose this, as is often said?

No. I was there too. I mean, one can certainly ask oneself whether or not corporate confessions of guilt are really something meaningful. But even I maintained that it is something quite proper that the Church, following the example of the Psalms and the Book of Baruch, should also confess her guilt through the centuries.

Did the idea to produce the Catechism of the Catholic Church *come from you?*

Not only me, but I was involved. More and more people asked themselves then: does the Church still have a homogeneous set of doctrines? They no longer knew what the Church actually believes. There were some very strong tendencies, with really good people onside too, saying: a catechism cannot be produced any more. I said: either we still have something to say, in which case one must be able to describe it – or we have nothing left to say. In this way I made myself a champion of the idea, with the conviction that we must be in a position to say what the Church believes and teaches today.

Fides et ratio, *Faith and reason, the 1998 encyclical – how much input did Cardinal Ratzinger have into this? None at all, or a little?*

A little, sure. Let's say, ideas.

Do you have a favourite anecdote from your relationship with John Paul II?

When the Pope was in Munich on his first trip to Germany, I saw what an incredible itinerary he had, that he was continuously busy from first thing in the morning till last thing at night. Then I thought to myself: This really shouldn't be done! You have to introduce a little rest. I then ensured there would be a nice lunchbreak. We had a lovely apartment in the Palais. He had only just gone up there at lunchtime when he called me, saying I should come up quickly. When I came up, he had just prayed with his breviary. I said: 'Holy Father, you simply must rest now!' 'I can rest in eternity,' he said. I think that is very typical of him: I can rest in eternity. In the present he was always restless.

Which perhaps also applies to you a little. When I was able to interview you for the first time in November 1992, in any case, you frankly confessed that you were exhausted, tired, and would actually have liked to resign your office. But fresh vitality was to come.

In 1991 I had this brain haemorrhage, the effects of which were still very intense in 1992. The years 1991 to 1993 were somewhat onerous, I have to say: in terms of physical strength and psychological strength. Then, yes, I pulled myself together again.

As you so often did. When was the first time you asked for your dismissal?

I have to think about that earnestly. I pointed out to the Pope after my first Quinquennium [five years] in 1986 that my tenure was served. But he told me that wasn't the case. I then asked for it urgently in 1991. As I said, I had suffered a brain haemorrhage and was in a decidedly bad way. I said to him: 'I can't do any more now.' But the response was a 'No'.

And for the third time?

Before I could ask him about it he had already said: 'You don't need to tell me, you don't need to write to me, saying that you want to be set free; it will not be heard. As long as I am here, you must stay.'

Your stroke in 1991 – for fourteen days you lay in Pius XI Hospital in Rome? What actually happened?

Well, it was a brain haemorrhage, with the result that the left field of vision was truncated. I still saw with that eye, but only straight ahead, nothing on the sides, at the edges. That was actually the only symptom, along with the general exhaustion. But of course that's unpleasant enough.

Any symptoms left now?

I very slowly regained my sight somewhat in the left eye. But then the day came, in 1984 I think, when I had a kind of embolism too, which spread to the whole eye. I was in Maria Eck and went to the optician the very next day. It was already too late then, so my vision was very severely impaired. That was being treated for a long time, until finally – a third thing – macula [Macula lutea – also called 'yellow spot', a disease of the retina], so now I'm simply blind in the left eye.

Completely?

Yes. I don't even see light and dark.

In the Vatican you never belonged to any cliques. You have an aversion to cronyism. Has your keeping a distance from the apparatus of power not earned you lots of enemies?

I don't think so, actually. I've even had friends. Everyone knew that I don't do any politicking, and that inhibits hostility. People know: he's not dangerous.

As the guardian of the faith for a quarter of a century you influenced the pontificate of John Paul II like no other. But, viewed conversely, what was Wojtyla's contribution to Ratzinger's development?

That I learned to think more broadly, especially in the dimension of religious dialogue. We interacted closely on the moral encyclical and the catechism, particularly. In that connection, his broader vision and his more philosophical viewpoint certainly also expanded my own horizon.

Who decided that you should write the text on the Way of the Cross at the Colosseum for Good Friday 2005, in which you speak of the quantity of filth in the Church betraying Christ. Was that the Pope's idea?

That came from himself, yes. The Pope wanted that himself.

Had he commented to you on the text?

No more, no, because he was already too ill and too tired.

Countless millions of people remember his funeral, whether on television screens around the world, or directly on St Peter's Square, which had 3 to 5 million people on the fringes. The plain wooden coffin, the wind that drove through the pages of the Gospel lying on it, the touching ceremony, which you conducted. What did you feel? What went through your mind?

This death had intensely moved me, naturally, because we were very close. He was a decisive character for me. I'd seen him all through his path of suffering and I knew, when I visited him in Gemelli Hospital, that it could not last much longer. And of course you grieve deeply, when someone close departs. At the same time, I had the awareness that he is there. That he blesses us from his window in heaven, as I then said on St Peter's Square too. That wasn't just words. That genuinely came from an inward awareness that even today he sends blessings down, that he is there and that the friendship endures in a different way.

PART THREE

The Pope of Jesus Christ

II

Suddenly Pontifex

When Joseph Ratzinger emerged before the faithful on 19 April 2005 on the loggia of St Peter's Basilica as St Peter's 265th successor, he looked almost like a teenager. After the long suffering of his predecessor, people weren't accustomed to seeing a Pope not sitting in a wheelchair, who was able to recite texts fluently and to the end. The Popes passing the baton could not have been more different. One was mystical and Marian, the other learned and Christocentric. Here the actor, the man of gesture who wooed the stage. There, the shy 'worker in the vineyard of the Lord', the man of the Word, who wanted to renounce the prizing of mere effects over substance. He saw his primary task, in his own words, as to preserve the Word of God 'in all its greatness and purity, from every attempt at adaptation and adulteration'. For him, reform is first of all a matter of the inner purification of the Church.

Holy Father, what did you actually dream of doing, when you believed that your service was now finally at an end after the death of John Paul II?

As I've already said, that I could someday write books in peace.

Did you think that was realistic?

Absolutely.

Right at the beginning of the conclave, you warned in a sermon of a 'dictatorship of relativism' that considers the only ultimate criterion to be the individual and his desires. In this situation the Church must proclaim the truth of faith against all ideologies and passing fads. The thinking of many Christians has been increasingly shaken by the waves of the Zeitgeist, and thrown from one extreme to another. In such times, those who have a 'clear faith' in keeping with the Creed of the Church will be rewarded with the label of fundamentalism. Priests should continue to be inspired by a 'holy restlessness' to bring people to the gift of faith, namely, to 'the word which opens the soul to God's joy' and implants them ultimately into 'the friendship of Christ'.[1] The clerics and faithful in St Peter's Square reacted with tumultuous applause. Many thought this speech about relativism was a candidate's manifesto for promotion.

Not at all. As dean of the College of Cardinals I just had to give the sermon for this service. And I simply interpreted the Letter to the Ephesians, completely in line with the fixed text for that week. The text says that one should not let oneself be tossed this way and that by the waves of time and so on.[2] So this was the result of that reading, its subject was conveyed.

This was already the third conclave you'd witnessed. Was it different to the others?

[1] Homily of Joseph Cardinal Ratzinger, given during mass on 18 April 2005.
[2] See Ephesians 4.14.

Well, with the first two I was still among the young and little-known cardinals, a novice shooter, so to speak, and in that sense I was in a quiet position. Here I had the responsibility of dean of the College of Cardinals. That means you have to conduct the Pope's funeral, you have to manage the preparations and then even have a responsibility in the conclave itself. At the end, it is the dean who asks the one selected whether or not he accepts. Through a good twenty years in Rome I was no longer an unknown quantity, my position this time was different from before. And finally, I was now seventy-eight years old, which was of course reassuring. If the bishops stop at seventy-five, you cannot hoist a seventy-eight-year-old onto the chair of Peter.

It would not have been the first time.

But there wasn't this seventy-five-year cut-off point then. I thought to myself that if the rule is that a bishop stops at seventy-five, then you cannot let the Bishop of Rome begin at seventy-eight.

It's very difficult to imagine that you went into the conclave, and did not even think that your election could happen.

Of course I'd been mentioned a lot beforehand. But I really wasn't able to take it seriously. I thought it couldn't happen, that it was unreasonable. In that sense I was just so taken aback.

Was there a minute to consider whether or not you should really accept the vote?

Certainly, yes. Indeed, the whole time. But I simply knew then, somehow, that I couldn't just say no.

When did you think about what papal name you would have?

Over the course of the election days.

The election day?

Or was it only a day?

It was two days, Monday and Tuesday.

Yes, over the course of the election days. I still hoped that it was not to be. Whereas it had indeed already become apparent on the first day that it could possibly fall to me.

Then it came into my mind that Benedict XV – and beyond him St Benedict himself – is the right connection to make.

Why did you not name yourself John Paul III?

I felt that would be inappropriate, because a standard had been set there which I couldn't match. I could not be a John Paul III. I was a different character, cut from a different cloth; I had a different sort of charisma, or rather a non-charisma.

Suddenly: Christ's vicar on earth. What inner change was going on there?

Yes, there was the thought: no, I need still more help from him. One knows: I really am not that. But if he lays the yoke on my shoulders, he must also help me bear it.

You spoke of the cardinals' ballot as the falling of a 'guillotine'.[3] Did you regret that later?

---

[3] *Light of the World*, p. 3.

No, the feeling was just like that, a guillotine.

Is there a model Pope? Paul VI perhaps?

I would not say so. For me, the Popes of the twentieth century were all models, each in his own way. I knew that I could not be in any way similar, but that they had each been witnesses for me.

Your first days having taken this new office, what particular memories stay with you?

The first days? Going for lunch in Santa Marta, the Vatican guesthouse, with my brother, with the whole family, and friends. That was very beautiful and moving. Then the first visit I received, Kirill, who was still then 'foreign minister' in Russia [patriarch of the Russian Orthodox Church since 2009].

How much sleep did you need then?

I need lots of sleep, so seven, eight hours. Yes, and then I had great difficulty with the cufflinks. They even got me quite annoyed, so I thought that whoever invented them must be in the depths of purgatory. [Laughs]

You'd not worn cufflinks before?

Occasionally, but not normally, no.

It was said that as Pope you immediately changed tailor, as the earlier one made the robes too short.

No, that's not correct. I've used Euroclero from the beginning, but always Gammarelli too. Anything without Gammarelli is a no-go.

And the first survey of the residence?

Ah, yes. First we looked at the tower. Here in the Vatican Gardens there is an old fortress tower which Papa Giovanni [Pope John XXIII] had renovated as a residential building. When the Apostolic Palace had to be restored for structural reasons, John Paul II also lived there for a long while. It was suggested to me that I first take up my residence in there. But I didn't like it. In the first place I don't like that the rooms are in a semicircle. I want straight, normal, human rooms. In addition, there was also such a terrible wind blowing up there, so I said no, I'd rather stay in Santa Marta until I can move into the Palazzo.

Did you have the papal appartamento *redesigned to make it brighter and more pleasant?*

I had the carpeted floors taken up first, as I don't like them. A floor is a floor, and a carpet is a carpet, either/ or. Then it was somewhat more pleasant, yes. But it had already been arranged that it would be repainted, because that hadn't been done for a long time. This was only done during the summer holidays.

Why have you never really given up your old home?

That was not intentional. I could not just give it up, because the move happened in great haste. I only had books brought over, otherwise virtually nothing practical. So everything was still there, even most of the books. At some point I thought: now we have to clear the place, but where will we actually put everything? But it was said to me: let it stay there for now.

So you weren't preparing for the worst?

No. It was perfectly clear to me that I could not go back there. Because even if I were to resign I could not live in a normal apartment; you can't.

As a great lover of music, do you work with music playing, for example while writing?

I would find it a disturbance. Either music or writing.

Do you need a particular atmosphere?

If I want to write or think, I only need silence. I must be able to be alone. I must concentrate on books in peace, then thoughts are able to ripen.

By the way, after your resignation was there a discussion about the papal household? It suddenly occurred to the Cardinal of Munich, Marx, that the 'court' was much too pompous. Was that your impression too?

Not at all, no. We always lived very simply, as I have from the beginning of my life. I am, so they would say, a *Hufschlager* [someone from the Hufschlag region where Ratzinger spent his childhood and youth]; for this reason alone I can't go for the court style. What prompted the cardinal to make his remark, I do not know.

Is there someone who briefed you in taking office? It's a truism that you can't teach a Pope.

[Laughs] Of course you can learn from the relevant officials, from the Cardinal Secretary of State or from assistants and so on. In that way one can gradually learn things somehow.

The first times we saw you, you often had rings under your eyes.

So?

It was obvious that your new tasks included very little sleep and lots of work.

I didn't feel bad in myself, but it's correct that from the beginning the load was almost overwhelming, and you just have to get used to it in order to remain in such a role.

12

Aspects of the Pontificate

Soon after the election of the German Pope, his smooth transition from the 'Pope of the Millennium', John Paul II, was already being considered something sensational. On the basis of the worldwide enthusiasm he received, commentators spoke of a '*Benedetto* fever'. Never before had so many people attended papal audiences. Benedict's encyclicals were reaching astronomically high numbers of editions. His speeches filled the front pages of the world's press.

On 24 April 2005, at the Papal Inauguration Mass to herald the new papacy, Benedict XVI said that 'the real programme of governance' is 'not to do my own will, not to pursue my own ideas, but to listen, together with the whole Church, to the word and the will of the Lord, to be guided by Him'. He went on: 'we are not some casual and meaningless product of evolution. Each of us is the fruit of a thought of God. Each of us is willed, each of us is loved, each of us is necessary.'

Holy Father, when and where did you actually write the great sermon of your inaugural mass? In your old apartment perhaps?

I can't remember exactly now. I think it was in Santa Marta.

You hadn't already considered previously what—

That's not permissible; one must trust in the inspiration of the moment.

The first speech or sermon of a new Pope is considered by the public to be the articulation of a programme. Did you see it that way too?

I was certainly aware it would be seen this way. Then I tried to write it together with God's help.

For over two decades you were the closest collaborator of a Pope, and for half your life you have concerned yourself theologically with the Petrine Primacy. Was there anything in particular that you were resolved not *to do?*

There was primarily the positive resolution that I wanted to put God and faith at the centre. It was also important to me to put Holy Scripture in the foreground. I was a man who came from a theological background, and I knew that my strength, if I have one, is to proclaim the faith positively. So above all I wanted to teach things from the fullness of Holy Scripture and Tradition.

To ask again: it is not only the things one does which are important, sometimes the things one does not *do are yet more significant.*

What should I say? I knew this would be no long pontificate. That I couldn't see any long-term projects to amend, and there'd be no kind of spectacular initiatives. Especially nothing like calling a new Council; but I could strengthen the synodal element more, and I wanted to do that.

Is it not also a problem if the follower of Peter the fisherman is a professor? In Jesus' selection of the twelve not a single scribe was called.

That's right, but there have been popes who were scholars, from Leo the Great and Gregory the Great in the beginning – two very great lights – then Innocent III, and so on. So it is not unusual either. Of course a Pope does not have to be a theological scholar, absolutely not. But he must have some cultivation of the intellect. He must know what the currents of the day are, the issues, the tasks, and in this sense, although being a professor is certainly not an ideal occupation for the episcopal or papal chair, it is not an impossibility either. OK, one only realizes afterwards that a professor is accused of approaching the contexts of life too theoretically, which is a danger when it comes to action. But he is gradually schooled in dealing with practical matters by the people around him, and this enables him to become something different; less theoretical and more capable of grasping practical tasks.

Cardinal Kurt Koch said that Pope Benedict had to take on and work on many problems, which were there before him, as legacies so to speak. Do you see it that way?

Certainly, and that's also the case now. There are always problems in the Church, certainly in our era as well, after the great upheavals of the post-Conciliar period, the whole confusion surrounding the question of how the Council should actually be read. On the whole, the situation in our society is such that Christianity must orientate itself afresh, define itself, realize itself. In that sense there were problems then, and there always will be.

Cardinal Koch also particularly meant problems which were not tackled under John Paul II, which were lying dormant.

There were some of course. But I would say that the Pope tackled what he could tackle. New issues arise again and again, and you can never tackle them all.

You assumed, as mentioned, that due to your old age you did not have a long period in office ahead of you. This awareness influenced your pontificate. Was it a mistake to adjust your plans to this assumption? You would have been able to proclaim a time of reform, and at least appoint the respective commissions.

Everyone has different charisms. Francis is a man of practical reform. He was archbishop for a long time, he knows the profession, and before that he was already a superior with the Jesuits, and he simply has the courage to organize things too. I knew that that was not my forte. And it wasn't necessary either, because there was John Paul II's reform of the Curia, *Pastor bonus.* To turn everything on its head so promptly did not seem right to me. It's correct that I couldn't take charge of any big, long-term organizational projects, but I deemed that it wasn't the right moment.

The former nuncio, Karl Josef Rauber, who you already knew from the Council, said about you: 'Joseph Ratzinger is a scholar of absolute integrity, but he is only interested in researching and writing.'

[Laughs] No, of course that's not right. That wouldn't work. You just have to do lots of practical things, and they bring joy. Visiting parishes, speaking to people, giving catechesis, leading all kinds of meetings. The parish visits are an especially lovely component; they make you happy. I was never a professor only. A priest cannot be just a professor by any means. If he were, he would be neglecting his calling. The priestly commission always involves some pastoral care, some liturgy too, as well as conversations. Maybe I have thought too much and written too much, that might well be. But it would not be the truth to say that that's all I've done.

That's right. Because it starts with a bang when you're the first Pope of the modern era to substitute the powerful symbol of the papal tiara with a simple bishop's mitre. Was there resistance in the College of Cardinals?

Not that I heard about. No one expressed any opposition directly, in any case. It was a change that was due, because if you no longer wear the tiara, it has to be replaced on the coat of arms.

Even besides that, the pontificate soon built momentum. For the first time at a synodal discussion, delegates from other confessions were invited. You established regular meetings with every head of the dicasteries[1], thereby reducing the audiences, trips, liturgical celebrations and canonizations. But you also broke with the previous Pope's practice of having guests at morning mass and taking meals with visitors.

From one perspective that was, of course, a deficiency on my part, but I must say, it couldn't have been otherwise. With Holy Mass in the morning, I needed silence

[1] A 'dicastery' is a department of the Roman Curia with a specific remit, a ministry in the governmental structure of the Church, such as the Congregation for Bishops or the Pontifical Council.

and recollection. I am not capable of plunging into meetings right at the beginning of the day. I simply need that quiet, so then I celebrated the mass without a big group of guests and could pray silently afterwards. That did not exclude other people from attending mass, but to have new faces, new encounters each day, and always in different languages too, that would have been too much for me. And similarly, after the day's meetings, I needed quiet during mealtimes. I simply couldn't continue making conversation then too.

There was an early change in switching the master of ceremonies from Piero Marini to Guido Marini. The exchange was interpreted to mean you wanted a different form to the papal services.

No, he was and is a very good man. OK, he is more liturgically progressive than I, but that doesn't matter at all. But he was of the opinion himself that it was time to end his role. So it turned out that after Marini 1, Marini 2 followed.

You had a different pastoral cross to your predecessor, of course, and wore the red cape instead of just the plain white cassock, and practised communion on the tongue. Critics said all this was a 'recourse to the liturgical rites of the past'. Was it that?

No. I was glad about the Council's reform, when it had been adopted honestly, and well, and in its authentic essence. However, there was much spin and lots of corruptions that one had to put a halt to. The liturgy in St Peter's was always good, and we tried to carry it on that way too. Communion on the tongue is not mandatory, I've always done both. But since there are so many people on St Peter's Square who might misunderstand that, who might pocket the host for example, it seemed to me to be entirely the right signal. But that I somehow operated in a restorative way? On the whole, I must say the liturgy is not ensnared in the categories of 'old' and 'new'. The Eastern Churches speak simply of the Divine Liturgy which we do not 'do', but which is a gift to us. J. A. Jungmann coined the expression 'becoming liturgy' for the Western context.[2] He pointed thereby to the stronger historical consciousness here in the West, where the liturgy grows and matures, experiences decay and renewal, but also has a continuity which is given by the Lord and the Apostolic Tradition. I have celebrated the liturgy from this awareness.

Were you resolved that Angelo Sodano would not stay Cardinal Secretary of State?

He was as old as me. And if the Pope is already old when he is elected, the Secretary of State must be operating at full force. He also saw it this way himself; that, by analogy, what applies to a normal bishop also applies to the Secretary of State. And if normal bishops resign at seventy-five or seventy-seven, the Secretary of State must also resign at least before he is eighty.

You had your first major international appearance with World Youth Day in Cologne, with a million participants. People saw the Pope laughing and singing, hand in hand with young people from all continents. Did you surprise yourself with your new style, your new radiance?

---

[2] Jungmann, J. A., *Gewordene Liturgie*, Innsbruck: Rauch, 1941.

In some ways, certainly. But I must mention that as a curate I very happily worked with young people. And as a professor you don't only read aloud to young people, you have a lot to do with them in practice. The company of young people was therefore not something alien to me. The World Youth Days are really numbered among some of the most beautiful memories of my whole pontificate. Cologne, Sydney, Madrid, these are three turning points in my life that I will never forget. I'm just joyful that I was able to be there, that I was accepted, and that I could help others.

All the detractors were silenced. For four years your pontificate was accompanied by an intense sense of excitement about the Pope from Bavaria. A first turning point was the commotion surrounding the famous 'Regensburg Speech'. A remark on the role of violence in Islam, made by the Byzantine Emperor Manuel II Palaiologos during a discussion with a Persian scholar, and which you quoted in your speech at the university, unleashed violent protests by Muslims across the world, angered that this quote was torn from its context.[i] We've already spoken about it at length in Light of the World.[3] *One last question on this cluster of issues: was it an accident that you stumbled upon this quote?*

I had read this dialogue of the Palaiologos because I was interested in Islamic–Christian dialogue. In that sense it was no accident. It really is about a dialogue. The emperor who was quoted already operated under general Muslim rule – and nevertheless there was a freedom, so he could say things people today are not able to

[3] See *Light of the World*, pp. 97ff.

say any more. As such, I just found it very interesting to bring up this part of a five-hundred-year-old dialogue for discussion. As already mentioned, I underestimated the political implications of the event.

And to clarify yet one more point: the Vaticanist Marco Politi wrote that Cardinal Sodano had already pointed out the explosive nature of the text even before the trip to Bavaria. You threw caution to the wind all the same. Is that right?

No. No one had said anything about it.

From this misrepresentation, Politi then deduces that the 'Scandal of Regensburg' had not just been an accident. You had performed a U-turn from Wojtyla's politics on the question of Muslim dialogue. As evidence he cites the fact that in the inaugural mass you deliberately left the Muslims without a mention.

That's not true. I know nothing about this accusation.

So neither is it true that you wanted to perform a U-turn from your predecessor's politics?

No. Not in the least.

After you had made access to the earlier, Latin form of the mass easier with your Motu Proprio Summorum Pontificum, *a discussion about the Good Friday prayer for the conversion of the Jews arose. You then replaced the text with a new formulation in February 2008. Was the controversy unavoidable?*

That was constructed by people who weren't friends of mine on the German theological scene. It was like this: we know the new Good Friday prayer, and it is accepted by everyone.[ii] But we had since then, even with John Paul II, taken into the Church a few groups with the old liturgy – the Fraternity of St Peter, for example. There were also a few communities of religious, and communities of the faithful, that celebrated with the old liturgy, including the old Good Friday Liturgy, a fact which was really not reckoned with. So I was surprised that nothing had been done about it.

I was of the opinion that one cannot let that go on, that even those using the old liturgy must change at this point in time. One had to have a form of the prayer created that fitted with the spiritual style of the old liturgy, but which was at the same time consonant with our modern understandings of Judaism and Christianity. The renewed Good Friday prayer, like all the prayers of Good Friday, consists in an invitation to pray, and the actual supplication. I quoted the invitation to pray verbatim from the intercessions of the Book of Hours. The actual supplication is composed of Scriptural texts. There is absolutely nothing contained in it which justifies the accusations that are perpetually rehashed in Germany.

I'm still happy today that I managed to change the old liturgy for the better at that moment. If one withdrew this new formulation of the supplication, as is always demanded, this would mean that the old, unacceptable, text with the *perfidi Iudaei* would have to be prayed. But certain people in Germany have always attempted to bring me down. They knew that this is easiest where Israel is concerned, and then they concocted these lies, saying God knows what was in this prayer. I have to say I think this is outrageous. Until then the old intercession was prayed, and I replaced it with a better one for this circle of people. But they didn't want anyone to understand that.

We've also spoken extensively about the abuse scandal in Light of the World.[4] *You only recently wrote an open letter which newly confronted the charge that you hushed things up in terms of abuse. Why was it so important to you to set the record straight once again?*

Because it was about the truth, and it would be disastrous if this slander were true. As Prefect of the Congregation for the Doctrine of the Faith, I immediately took matters in hand when they came to me. At first the Congregation for the Clergy had claimed jurisdiction. But I saw that the strict line on it which was necessary would not be taken, and I brought it under the CDF's remit. I was aware that it was a very difficult task, and that we would experience criticism, but I also knew that we had people who were better able to master it. The fact that the CDF were dealing with it would also be a signal that this task has the highest priority for the Church.

In your aforementioned text on the Way of the Cross from 2005 you speak of 'filth' in the Church. Does that word refer then already to the cases of abuse?

It was involved. But I thought of so many things. As Cardinal of the CDF one hears of so many things, because all the scandals arrive there, so one really needs a strong soul in order to bear everything. One always knows that filthy things are going on in the Church,

[4] See *Light of the World*, pp. 18ff.

but what one has to stomach as head of the CDF is really very far-reaching, and in that connection I simply wanted to pray to the Lord himself, so that he helps us.

Many believe that John Paul II did not tackle this problem vigorously enough.

It always depends on the information. When he was sufficiently informed and saw what was going on, he was wholly convinced that it had to be tackled energetically. Under the existing Church law it was not possible to dole out the most severe punishments. I said then that we needed new amendments. The Pope immediately gave me a free rein on this. We created new legal norms and structures, just so that the issue could be dealt with.

Your predecessor called for the New Evangelization, but it was really helped on its way by your pontificate, particularly through establishing the Pontifical Council for Promoting New Evangelization. It is, however, likely to take centuries to Christianize the continent of Europe again, if this is possible at all. Are you not deluding yourself there?

It is not permissible simply to give up proclaiming the gospel. Indeed, it seemed completely absurd in ancient times that a couple of Jews went out and sought to win the great, learned and knowledgeable Graeco-Roman world for Christianity. There will always be great failures too. We do not know how Europe will develop, or the degree to which it will still be Europe if different strata of the population newly structure it. But to proclaim this Word, which bears power in itself, to build the future which makes the lives of human beings meaningful, that is independent of any calculation of success, and absolutely necessary. The Apostles could not make sociological investigations, that happens or it doesn't, but they had to trust in the inner power of this Word. At first, very few, lowly, people joined. But then the circle grew.

Of course the Word of Gospel can disappear from continents. Indeed we can see now that the Christian continents of the beginning, Asia Minor and North Africa, are no longer Christian. It can even disappear in places where it was dominant. But it can never remain unsaid; will never be unimportant.

Now to the reauthorization of the Tridentine Mass. This endeavour was somewhat timid. Was that because of the resisters within the Church itself?

Sure, first because there was a fear of, let's say, the restoration, and, second, some people who simply misunderstood the reform. It was certainly not as though there would now be another mass. There are two ways to represent it ritually, but they belong to one fundamental rite. I have always said, and even still say, that it was important that something which was previously the most sacred thing in the Church to people should not suddenly be completely forbidden. A society that considers now to be forbidden what it once perceived as the central core – that cannot be. The inner identity it has with the other must remain visible. So for me it was not about tactical matters and God knows what, but about the inward reconciliation of the Church with itself.

The reauthorization of the Tridentine Mass is often interpreted primarily as a concession to the Society of St Pius X.

That is just absolutely false! It was important for me that the Church is one with herself inwardly, with her own past; that what was previously holy to her is not somehow wrong now. The rite must develop. In that sense reform is appropriate. But the continuity must not be ruptured. The Society of St Pius X is based on the fact that people felt the Church was renouncing itself. That must not be. But as I said, my intentions were not of a tactical nature, they were about the substance of the matter itself. Of course it is also the case that, the moment one sees a Church schism looming, the Pope is obliged to do whatever is possible to prevent it happening. This also includes the attempt to lead these people back into unity with the Church, if possible.

As Prefect you complained about an impoverishment and a misuse of the liturgy. The liturgy is the pivot and fulcrum of the faith, the future of the Church depends on it. If so, why has so little happened in this area? You certainly had all the authority to do something.

Institutionally and juridically one cannot do much about it at all. What is important is that an inward vision emerges, and that people learn what liturgy is from seeing inwardly – learn what it really means. That is why I've just written books. Unfortunately there are still, in today's confined spaces, certain groups of supposed experts who absolutize their theories and do not see what the essential thing is. It is not about allowing any kind of private gimmicks, but rather that the liturgy fulfils the Church, and is celebrated from within. But one cannot just command that.

One thinks a Pope has the authority; he can put his foot down.

No.

It won't work?

It won't work, no!

In ecumenism many initiatives emerged in your pontificate, but many remained without an echo. What disappointed you the most about the ecumenical process?

I have been difficult to disappoint there, because I am simply familiar with the reality and know what one may and may not expect concretely. The situation between us and the Protestants and us and the Orthodox is very different. The obstacles are also very different. With the Protestants, I would say the internal disagreements are the really big problem. One is always speaking only to a partial reality, which then excludes another partial reality. They themselves are in a major crisis, as we know. Of course you can be disappointed. But whoever knows the reality cannot expect that Church unity is coming, in the genuine sense of the word. One has to strive for it, that we ever more listen and learn from each other, so the essential thing is not lost, faith in Jesus Christ the Son of God, and from here the fundamental directions for practical activities emerge.

But at the beginning you spoke very hopefully of concrete and visible signs of a reunification.

Compared with before, we have certainly made headway. On the other hand, the Protestant Church in Germany is in a great crisis. Where is it going? What can you modernize? What must stand firm? There are opposing forces. There are forces which are already very close to us, and others going very far away from us.

Regarding the relationship to Orthodoxy in Russia, it looked intermittently as if a meeting between the Pope and the Moscow Patriarch could be possible while you were still in office.

Yes. Indeed. There is a certain personal affection there, which I've already indicated, and also a shared knowledge of Christian essentials, and because of that, an understanding that we must hold firm to the great, moral insights too, to marriage and the family and so on. There is great common ground. This was particularly apparent to people in Russia, who experienced the outcomes of what happens when you lose sight of that. On the other hand, the historical and institutional burdens are in turn so large that one must be very cautious with concrete hopes.

Above all the very positive development of the relationship between Rome and Byzantium must be mentioned here. Between the churches of Rome and Constantinople a truly fraternal relationship is developing. Patriarch Bartholomew I is not only a man of exceptional education, but a real man of God. I am happy and grateful that we have joined into a truly personal friendship. He has even already visited me here in my little monastery.

The foremost event of your pontificate was the publication of your three-volume work about Jesus Christ, which will probably be the basic text of Christian faith for generations of priests and laypeople. Because, for the first time in history, here a Pope presented a decidedly theological study on the founder of the Church. The work reached millions of readers around the world, and marked a turning-point in the treatment of the Gospels, and the way they are dealt with. You leave no doubt as to their authenticity, and you interpret their assertions afresh for the contemporary world. The project had already originated before the pontificate. Did you even consider the question of whether or not it is right for a Pope to write books?

I just knew that I had to write it. In that sense I never had any doubt that I'm allowed to write it.

The first volume appeared on your eightieth birthday in 2007. How on earth did you find any time for this work?

I ask myself that question too. The loving God particularly helped me with that. But it was something close to my heart that I could still be able to pull it off. Because, as with the liturgy – which as the self-awareness of the Church is central, so if the liturgy ceases to be itself, this is lost – so it is with Jesus; if we no longer know Jesus, the Church is finished. And the danger that we will just destroy him and talk him to death with certain types of exegesis is overwhelming. Therefore I had to get a bit stuck in to the battles over the details. It is not sufficient just to interpret the texts spiritually with dogma. One must enter into the disputes, and do so indeed without losing oneself in the exegetical details, but go far enough to recognize that the historical method does not prohibit faith.

Were you assisted in writing it?

No. I have always kept abreast of the theological scene, and continually followed the debates and discoveries, so I had also done the preparation with that.

And after carrying out your official duties, were you able to sit down and just continue writing where you left off? As when someone picks up some knitting again and just carries on knitting?

[Laughs] Something like that. With an issue that I have inwardly concerned myself with so much, which is so present to me, when I plug myself into it, so to speak, it immediately resumes.

When someone undertakes such a big project at eighty years old, and occupies himself intensely with a topic that he's been concerned about his whole life – how does an author do that?

First, you have to read everything and think about it afresh once again. On the one hand, with the texts of the Gospels; on the other, in conversation with the most important exegetical works. Through that you learn it afresh once again. Intellectual progress had been made when I had got down into the details, and was able to say what I had to say. Because it is only when you can express it and say it that you have inwardly understood it.

When it affects the person very strongly again?

Definitely. It comes close to you as something completely new. Because you've thought everything through thoroughly again. The eschatological discourse of Jesus, for example, where everyone thought that the world was ending with Jerusalem.[5] Or even with the issue of the atonement. To find a way in here, to these such difficult points. And I found that then, when I thought I had the fundamental insights, new things were given to me again.

Could one say that this work was an irreplaceable source of strength for your pontificate?

Certainly. It was for me the perpetual wellspring from the depths of the sources.

Was there ever a second of your life when you asked yourself whether or not everything we believe about God is only an idea? Whether you might wake up one day and say: Yes, we were wrong?

The question 'is it really proven?' comes to one again and again. But then I've had so many concrete experiences of faith, experiences of the presence of God, that I am ready for these moments and they cannot crush me.

And there's never been a crisis of faith? In your youth, in your student years, for example?

Then least of all. Then the Church was still so living, everything still so simple and straightforward, true and reconciled. No, only later, as the world has become so fragmented, Christianity, the Church itself, no longer seemed to know who she is. But I have indeed always been held firm. Thanks be to God.

---

[5] For a classic example of one of Jesus' eschatological discourses, see Mark 13.

There were 'only' three encyclicals in your pontificate. Why were you so sparing there?

First, because I just wanted to finished the Jesus book. Here one can of course say my priorities were wrong. But it is a reason in any case. And then also, after the great wealth of encyclicals bequeathed to us by John Paul II, I believed that I should now strike a slower rhythm.

Do you have a favourite encyclical? Which is your favourite?

Yes, indeed, maybe the first, *Deus caritas est*.

13

Journeys and Encounters

Let us turn to a few encounters with prominent contemporaries. Did you meet Václav Havel?

Yes, that was really pleasant. I'd read a few things by him, which really hit the bullseye. Just what he said about the relationship between politics and truth. He was already unwell, but it was just so moving for me to speak with the man Václav Havel. Then the meeting with Shimon Peres was also a major encounter for me; he's a figure I admire. We know how his father perished. He is inwardly so, yes, kind, and continually open, with such a sincere humanity and generosity of spirit.

How was it with Obama?

A great politician of course, who knows what it takes to be successful, and has certain ideas that we cannot share, but he was not only a tactician to me, but certainly a reflective man too. I felt that he sought the meeting between us, and that he listened. Incidentally, there is also Michelle Bachelet, the president of Chile, who is an atheist, Marxist, and in that sense at variance with us on many things. But somehow I saw in her a fundamental ethical will, which comes close to the Christian will. It was a good conversation. I got to know these people, and not only from their political and tactical sides. What was generally impressive about these encounters was discerning that – although these people indeed think very differently to us on many issues – they certainly try to see what is right.

You gladly spoke with agnostics, professed atheists, with left-wingers.

Yes, yes, sure, that is somehow necessary. If they think and speak honestly. Of course there are fanatics, who are only functionaries and just dispense their working slogans. But if they are human beings, one can see that they are somehow restless inside . . .

Have you visited Jürgen Habermas again, with whom you held a famous philosophical debate at a meeting in Munich?

I haven't seen him since. But he sent me a postcard from a trip, and then somehow a little connection has remained.

How was the meeting with Putin?

Very interesting. We spoke with each other in German; he speaks perfect German. We didn't go very deep, but I certainly believe that he is – a man of power of course – somehow affected by the necessity of faith. He is a realist. He sees how Russia suffers from the destruction of morality. Even as a patriot, as someone who wants Russia to have great power again, he sees that the destruction of Christianity threatens to destroy Russia. A human being needs God, he sees that quite evidently, and he is certainly affected by it inwardly as well. He has now even, as he gave the *Papa* [Pope Francis] an icon, made the sign of the cross and kissed it . . .

Someone with whom you could obviously get on well was Giorgio Napolitano, the then Italian president and a former communist . . .

Yes, we have a genuine friendship. I had already had a great friendship with Francesco Cossiga [President of Italy 1985–1992] previously, and with Carlo Azeglio Ciampi [President of Italy 1999–2006]; Napolitano is a man to whom what matters is justice and what is right and good, not the success of the party. We understand each other really quite well. He has also already visited me here in the monastery.

What was the most sensitive visit?

The most sensitive visit was perhaps the one to Turkey. There was still this cloud hanging in the air after the Regensburg Speech. That's why Erdogan didn't want to meet me at first. The atmosphere gradually warmed up, so that by the end there was genuine agreement there. But it was sensitive at the beginning, and I am therefore very grateful to the loving God that hearts somehow opened up on both sides.

On 18 April 2008 you give the now famous speech to the UN in New York. The New York Times *wrote that: 'whoever isn't touched by this is no longer alive'. And* The Times *of London wrote: 'With his journey to the United States of America, Pope Benedict has without doubt stepped out of the*

shadow of his predecessor and has shown his own charisma.'
How was it for you?

In the General Assembly it was, first, impressive to experience the great attentiveness which lasted for the whole duration of my speech. And it seemed to me that the standing ovation was also an expression of the fact that the speech had really touched people. Afterwards, there was a wealth of encounters with human beings of different origins, with children, with UN staff, and politicians. Here, the UN portrayed itself not as an institution but as a community of human beings, no longer purely anonymous and institutional, but rather composed of persons. All these persons were also very pleased that the Pope was there at the UN and had come to speak with them.

Paris, 12 September 2008: your appearance in the French capital was like a football team playing a home match. You seemed to feel particularly comfortable.

I have to say yes. I love French culture and I am very at home in it somehow. It was really lovely, just the large mass on the Esplanade des Invalides, two hundred thousand people—

Something no one thought possible—

—the meeting in the Academy, where we were simply together like friends, that was really very moving. Then the meeting at the Collège des Bernardins, where the former presidents were. Giscard knew me, he visited me once again afterwards. I had worked out my contributions to the French theological tradition, so that the intellectual connection was present, so to speak, from their own interiority.

Paris – many memories of this place must be coming back to you.

Although I wasn't there as often as you'd think. The first time was 1954, for a big conference on Augustine, which was the first major foreign trip I'd ever made. To be in the world of international academic inquiry, and specifically in the intellectual world of the French, stays with me as the memory *par excellence.*

Let us come to a difficult visit, although it was your homeland: Berlin, September 2010. I suppose this trip was a particular challenge for you.

Very much so, for the very reason that, in many respects, Berlin is somehow different to the Catholic tradition, and the city is an expression of the Protestant world. Catholicism is indeed there, and it is lived too, but it is somehow marginal. Romano Guardini, in his letters to Fr Weiger, which Barbara Gerl-Falkowitz published, depicts in an exhilarating way how he was left even physically dejected and shaken by the force of profane culture in contrast to the poverty of Catholicism in Berlin.[1] This was certainly a first impression, which has slowly corrected itself somewhat. But the basic orientation was confirmed again. So it's clear that one could not expect that Berlin would be like Madrid, or even like London or Edinburgh. There are other cities which are not at all Catholic, but the people are somehow different there . . .

People who just a year before had received the Pope enthusiastically.

[1] Published in English as Romano Guardini, *Letters from Lake Como,* Michigan: Eerdmans, 1994.

Berlin is naturally cool in its manner. But yes, the Catholics have also shown that they are happy and just that they are there. The service at the Olympic Stadium was certainly impressive . . .

Were you prepared for something to happen there which you would not like?

The danger existed. We certainly knew that with *Papa Giovanni Paolo secondo* there were very bad disturbances there.

I'm not talking about protests on the street, but from representatives of society, of politics. Already in his welcoming speech, President Wulff made demands for change in Catholic principles.

One had to reckon with such things. In that sense it didn't at all surprise me or leave me dismayed. It was then very moving, how tense the atmosphere was during my speech in the Reichstag. The attentiveness was so intense you could have heard a pin drop. And it felt that this was not just a matter of courtesy, but a deeper sense of listening was there; that was then a significant moment for me.

In your great speech in Freiburg you called for the Church to detach itself from the world, which was necessary so that the faith can unfold its active potency again. It was not a call for people to turn away from Christian love or renounce social and political engagement, but to turn away from power, from Mammon, from false appearance, from deception and self-deception. The speech was widely misinterpreted, in part quite consciously, even by Church people. How is that even possible?

The phrase 'detachment from the world' is apparently quite alien to people; in that sense it was perhaps not wise to put the phrase so much in the foreground. But the message of the content was clear enough, and whoever wanted to understand it could understand it.

It was a revolutionary message.

Certainly.

It was about remaining resistant, uncomfortable, unaccommodating, to show once again that Christianity is bound up with a worldview that reaches beyond everything involved in a purely secular, materialistic worldview, for it has the mystery of eternal life. It called for a new truthfulness and authenticity in Christian life, and so for the genuine, the decisive reform of the Church. Something which Pope Francis apparently understands very well.

Precisely, that is different.

To the question of the German church tax: would you have decided differently, if it was only up to you?

In fact I have great doubts about whether or not the church tax system is right, as it is. I don't mean whether there should be a tax system at all. But the automatic excommunication of those who don't pay, is, in my opinion, indefensible.

Much of the media in Germany regard the Catholic Church as an enemy of progress that must be opposed. Perhaps no Pope of the modern era has been treated so badly in his home-land as you were. How deeply did that affect you?

Now, the popes of the modern era were all Italians, which is not to forget how badly Pius IX was misunderstood when he was not willing to lead Italy into war with Austria. He was at first regarded as the patriotic, open-minded, modern Pope, but after he refused to meet this expectation, there was a total rejection. A rejection so radical it can hardly be imagined today. He did something great, because if he had let himself be made Italy's leader, the papacy would have come to an end. He underwent a plunge in public favour, which only a saint could withstand.

Benedict XV is another example. For the Italians, participating in the First World War was part of *Risorgimento*, the rebirth of Italy. Trent was still with Austria, it was yet to be part of Italy. So for the people there the First World War was a patriotic duty. And Benedict XV said the war was a senseless slaughter. This was met with the utmost resentment even by Catholics. But it was basically heroic to say: no, it is not a patriotic act, it is meaningless destruction.

In other words, placing the attacks directed at you against this background, they haven't affected you too—

No, precisely when I think of both these popes from the last and second-to-last centuries, Pius IX and Benedict XV. They experienced it in extreme ways, and much more terribly than I.

The Catholic establishment also attracted attention in Germany less from social engagement than from things like the New Evangelization, even if the loss of faith in this country has reached dramatic proportions.

In Germany we have this established and well-paid Catholicism, often with employed Catholics, who then oppose the Church with a trade-union mentality. For them the Church is only an employer towards whom they are critical. They don't approach matters from a dynamic of faith, but rather from just this sort of position. This, I believe, is the great danger threatening the Church in Germany: that she has so many paid employees, and therefore a surplus of non-spiritual bureaucracy. The Italians cannot afford nearly as many employees, so participation is based mainly on voluntary work. In this way, for example, regular, large meetings of Catholics in Rimini were completely built up on conviction. Everything that has to happen there, converting the halls, the functioning of the technology, is done by volunteers, unpaid. That is a different situation.

And creates a different mindset.

Of course. I'm saddened by this situation, this excess of money, which then again is something too little, and the bitterness which is growing about it, the malice which is there in German intellectual circles.

How deep was your disappointment with your trip to Germany?

The word disappointment does not apply to my own assessment of the visit. Of course I was aware that the forces of this established Catholicism would not agree with what I said, but on the other hand my speech had caused some reflection, as well as inspiring silent forces within the Church and encouraging them. It is quite natural that such considerations would lead to some negative responses. Thoughtfulness, and the willingness for genuine renewal, are the genuinely essential things.

Havana, 28 March 2012. First you went to Mexico, then Havana. How do you remember your arrival in Havana?

Of course I know that everything was prescribed as apparatus of a state visit, the big artillery, the gunfire, but somehow it also felt like a recognition of the Pope and the papacy, the Church and Christianity, which gives hope.

I had proposed that even Cuba should make Good Friday a holiday. Raúl Castro said: 'That's beyond me, only the Council of State can do it. I can do it this year as an exception, and then it goes through the Council of State.' So it happened. I had the impression that it is important to him, to come away without a break, as it were, from rigid Marxist theory, while the authority of the state remains in existence, but the openness to Christianity grows. And therefore freedom grows too.

How did you find the meeting with Fidel Castro?

It was touching, somehow. He is of course old and unwell, but certainly very with it and he has vitality. I don't think he has, on the whole, yet come out of the thought-structures by which he became powerful. But he sees that through the convulsions in world history, the religious question is being posed afresh. He even asked me to send him some literature.

Did you do it?

I sent him *Introduction to Christianity*, and one or two other things too. He is not a person with whom one must expect a major conversion, but a man who sees that things have gone differently, that he has to think and ask questions about the whole again.

14

Shortcomings and Problems

Holy Father, you made a Protestant President of the Pontifical Academy of Sciences. Under you, there was for the first time a Muslim professor at the Gregorian, who teaches the Qur'an. Under your leadership, the Pontifical Council for the New Evangelization was formed, the organizational basis for the mission to the modern world. You created the possibility for other denominations, for example the Anglicans, to live within the Catholic Church with their own traditions. In the scope of this conversation, we can address only a partial segment of the wealth of decision and events of your pontificate. I would therefore like to shed some light on those things which commentators have brought to the table, not in support of your leadership but against it. One of the reproaches is that you were too little prepared to make changes.

One must say first of all that in a pontificate which begins when one is seventy-eight years old, one should not strive for great, wide-ranging perspectives aimed at making changes which one cannot then see through oneself. I've said that already. One must do what is possible in the moment. And second, what would be considered as major changes? The important thing is that the faith endures today. I see this as the central task.

All the rest is just administrative issues, which it was not necessary to unleash during my tenure.

Did you not see the need for a push to modernize the Catholic Church?

It depends on how 'a push to modernize' is understood. The question is not what is modern and who is modern. What is important in fact is not only that we proclaim the faith in true and good forms, but that we understand it anew for the present world, and learn to express it newly, and then shape a new way of living too. But that happened as well. Through providence, through the Holy Spirit, through the young religious movements. In these movements there are forms which portray the life of the Church in new ways. If, for example, I compare the sisters here in the *monasterio*, the Memores sisters, with the sisters from the past, I can discern a great push to modernize. Simply because in a place, where faith is active and living, where it is not living in negation but in joy, new forms are found too.

This is what makes me joyful: that the faith depicts itself afresh in young movements, and the Church gains a new countenance here. This is something you see primarily at the World Youth Days. You don't see a sort of people there who have lagged behind the times, but young people who feel that we need something different from the usual watchwords. They really set things alight. John Paul II initiated these things, building up a new generation, acquiring a young, fresh face for the Church.

You demanded early on that the Church separate herself from some goods, so that her true Good comes into play. Didn't this slogan of your pontificate need to be followed up with clearer signs and deeds?

Maybe, but it is very difficult. There, one must always begin with oneself. Does the Vatican possess too much? I don't know. We must do a great deal for the poor countries who need our help. But there is South America, there is Africa, and so on. Money must be there above all for giving, for service. But it has to come in somehow, before you can give it away. So I don't really know what we could have given away. I believe that every local church should ask itself that, beginning in Germany.

What is happening now under Pope Francis is putting official Church things, which no longer suit the time, into question.

From the outset, the IOR [the Vatican bank Istituto per le Opere di Religione] was a big issue for me, and I tried to reform it. That doesn't happen quickly, because you have to become deeply acquainted with it. It was important to take it out of the hands it was in previously. It had to be found a new leadership, and it seemed right for many reasons not to appoint an Italian as the boss any more. I can say that with Baron Freyberg I had found a very good solution.[1]

Your idea?

Si. Added to this were the laws that were made under my responsibility, for example to put an end to

---

[1] Ernst von Freyberg was appointed President of the Board of Superintendence of the Istituto per le Opere di Religione by the Commission of Cardinals of the IOR on 15 February 2013. Baron von Freyberg left the IOR in July 2014.

money-laundering. This is well acknowledged internationally. Anyway, I did quite a lot to reform the IOR. I also strengthened the two international commissions, so that they should have more control and achieve clearer advances. Silently I worked on both the legislation and concrete things. I think this can now be built on and taken further.

During your pontificate things came to light that had long since been covered up.

Naturally I wanted to do more than I could. Because of the Ninth Station of the Cross [when the cardinal spoke about filth in the Church] many have said: Ah, the Pope, he will intervene now! I wanted to as well, but it is so difficult to find a way in. Structural and personal problems interlock with each other, and one can destroy more than heal by premature intervention. Therefore you can only go about it slowly and cautiously.

After your resignation it was admitted that you had dismissed hundreds of priests connected with abuse worldwide.

When the affair began, only suspension was possible by the penal law of the Codex [*Codex Iuris Canonici*, the Church's criminal law processes]. But that was totally inadequate by American law, because those concerned continued being priests. We then decided together with the American bishops: only if these priests are laicized is it made clear that we have punished them, if we dismiss them from priestly service.

You are still speaking about your time as Prefect.

Yes, yes, that's right. I then worked on the amendment to the criminal law, which was very weak in itself, above all in order to strengthen the protection of victims, and to be able to take a grip on things more quickly. Because the processes drag on endlessly, and if it's only after ten years that I'm able to punish someone, it is simply too late.

The dismissal of around four hundred priests . . .

That was as Pope, but on the basis of the law that we had created previously.

On the Williamson affair that we discussed at length in Light of the World.[i] *There is still another question to add: when exactly were you informed about the problem?*

Only after it had already happened, anyway. I do not understand, if it was so known about, how no one among us discerned it; that is inconceivable to me, incomprehensible.

Your Secretary of State, Cardinal Bertone, had asked if you would suspend the remittance.

Yes, sure.

It would have been no problem.

Of course, But I don't believe he knew[2]; I can't imagine that.

[2] The Pope Emeritus is confirming here that Cardinal Bertone was not aware of Richard Williamson's statement of Holocaust denial on Swedish television broadcast on 22 January 2009 and reported in *Der Spiegel* two days earlier. See Author's Notes p. 249.

The Williamson case can in a sense be regarded as the turning point of your pontificate. Do you see it as that as well?

There was then a huge propaganda campaign against me, naturally. The people who were against me finally had the tangible evidence to say that I was unfit and in the wrong place. In that regard it was a dark hour and a time that was difficult. But then people understood that I really had just not been informed.

Is it true that there weren't any personnel consequences?

No. In connection with it I completely reorganized the Ecclesia Dei commission, which was responsible here. Because I concluded from that case that it wasn't working properly.

Were you too soft?

I saw the blame as lying only at the door of this commission, and I thoroughly transformed it.

The writers Andrea Tornielli and Paolo Rodari come to the conclusion in their book Attacco a Ratzinger *[Attack on Ratzinger], which had been published before the Vatileaks affair, that there had been conspiracies, media campaigns and attacks against Pope Benedict, stemming from anti-Catholic circles. Did you feel with certain projects a resistance within the Curia too?*

No, I can't say I did. The important people, the prefects and presidents, all stood by me anyway.

Your Cardinal Secretary of State, Tarcisio Bertone, has especially come under heavy fire. Bertone did not come from the world of diplomacy. Under a professional manager of the Secretariat of State, the critics say, many deficiencies and shortcomings would not even have happened. These issues were then laid on your shoulders. Why didn't you put someone else into this important post?

Because I had no reason to. Bertone was certainly no diplomat, that is true; he was a pastor, a bishop and theologian, professor, canon lawyer. As a canonist he had lectured on international law, and was skilled in the legal aspects of the role. There was from the very start a strong prejudice against him coming from some quarters. Of course they have seized on every opportunity to have this confirmed. OK, perhaps he had some failures, too many trips etc. But who actually makes no mistakes? For me he is and remains a man of the faith who has tried to serve the Church rightly. Incidentally, legal investigations into individual problems are under way, whose outcomes we have to wait for.

Is it true that several cardinals, including Cardinal Schönborn, had called for Bertone's replacement at a meeting with you? The answer was, allegedly: 'Bertone remains – basta!'

No, that didn't happen.

Like your name patron, St Benedict, you were also confronted with a 'raven', as someone referred to your servant Paolo Gabriele, the thief of confidential files from your closest surroundings. How hard did this story hit you?

Not hard enough for me to collapse into some kind of despair or world-weariness, at least. It was simply unintelligible to me. Even when I see the person I can't understand how someone would want to do something like that – what can have been expected from it. I cannot penetrate this psychology.

Some say something like that was able to happen because of your excessive credulity.

Well, I didn't choose him. I didn't know him at all. He passed through the system, through all the tests. And from all sides he seemed to be the right man.

Knowledge of human nature, they say, was not generally your strong point.

[Laughs] Yes, I would certainly concede that. I am, on the other hand, very careful and cautious, because I have experienced the limits of human nature in others and, indeed, often experienced them with myself too.

How did you see the legal side to the case?

It was important to me that even in the Vatican the independence of the judiciary is preserved, that the sovereign does not say 'now I'm taking it into my own hands', but rather in a state under the rule of law the judiciary must have their way. Afterwards the sovereign can speak words of grace; that is a different matter.

Your former servant was sentenced to eighteen months' imprisonment on 6 October 2012 for serious theft. He entered the prison in the Vatican on 25 October. You visited him on 22 December, forgave him, and rescinded the serving of his remaining sentence. Gabriele was released the very next day. What did he impart to you during your visit?

He was shocked at himself. I would not like to analyse his personality. It's a strange lot that he has been given in life, or which he has given himself. He understood that that could not have been allowed, that he was simply on the wrong path.

There was speculation about whether a mere servant acting alone could see through an action of such magnitude at all. What do you think?

The passing on of the documents he certainly did alone. No one else could have been close enough.

But perhaps there were like-minded people, friends, who encouraged him?

There could have been, I don't know. Nothing has been found in any case.

To elucidate these things you established a separate independent commission. Did it not shock you that there is such a high level of envy, jealousy, careerism and intrigue in the Vatican?

Well, one knows that. I must say explicitly that everything is indeed there, but that is not the whole of the Vatican. There are so many genuinely good people who work with full dedication, from dawn to dusk. I know so many good apples that I have to say, well, one just has to suffer things like that too. In an organism with several thousand people it is impossible to have only sincere, good people. You have to concede the one side, with all the deplorability associated with it, but the other side should not be overlooked. It touches me how many people I meet here who, from their innermost selves, want to act and be there for God and for the Church and for human beings. How many kind, sincere people have I met here! That outweighs the other side for me, and I say, the world is simply like this! We know this from the Lord! The bad fish are also in the net.

To bring this cluster of issues to a close: your successor has spoken of a gay lobby in the Vatican, a homosexual clique. That was a problem. Did you see that too?

A group had been pointed out to me, in fact, which we have since dismantled. That was even revealed in the report of the tripartite commission[3] that was able to link a group of individuals, a small one, maybe four or five people, which we dismantled. Whether something forms again, I do not know. It would not be teeming with such things anyway.

Did the Vatileaks affair make you fatigued with being in office?

No, I mean, because that can always happen. Above all, as already said, one is not permitted to go in the moment of the storm, but must then stand firm.

---

[3] So called because it was supervised by three cardinals.

Conclusion

Pope Benedict, in the 1950s you predicted an enormous loss of faith across much of Europe. That won you a reputation as a pessimist. Today one sees how your vision of the 'small Church' which would lose many of her privileges, which would be opposed, and around which fewer and fewer believers in the strict sense would gather, has come true.

Certainly, yes. I would say the dechristianization continues.

How do you see the future of Christianity today?

That we're no longer coextensive with modern culture, the basic shape of Christianity is no longer determined, that is obvious. Today we live in a positivistic and agnostic culture, which shows itself more and more intolerant towards Christianity. In that sense, Western society, or Europe in any case, will no longer simply be a Christian society. Believers will have to strive all the more to continue to form and to bear the awareness of values and the awareness of life. A resolute faith among individual congregations and local churches will be important. The responsibility is greater.

In retrospect, what would you consider as the anchor of your pontificate, the hallmarks?

I would say that the 'Year of Faith' expresses it well: a new encouragement for faith, for a life from the centre, from vitality, to discover God again, to discover Christ again, and so find the centrality of faith again.

Do you see yourself as the last Pope of an old era or the first Pope of a new era?

Between the times, I would say.

As a bridge, a kind of connecting link between the two worlds?

I don't belong to the old world any more, but the new world isn't really here yet.

Is the election of Pope Francis perhaps the outward sign of a turning point between eras? Does a new era definitively begin with him?

You always recognize the divisions of eras only later: that the medieval age begins here at such-and-such a date, or modernity there. You only see in retrospect how the forces of history are proceeding. In that sense I would not venture to say that now. But it is obvious that the Church is increasingly stepping out of the old European fabric of life, and is thus taking on a new character and a new form in her trajectory. Above all, we see how the dechristianization of Europe progresses, that in Europe things pertaining to Christianity are increasingly disappearing from the character of public life. So the Church must find a new kind of presence, must change her way of being present. There are seismic periodic changes in process. But we do not yet know at which precise point we can say that one era begins and another starts.

You know the prophecy of Malachy, who in the Middle Ages predicted a list of future popes even to the end of time, at least the end of the Church. According to this list, the papacy ends after your pontificate. Is that an issue for you, whether it can actually be that at least you are the last of a series of popes, as we have known the office so far?

Anything can be. This prophecy probably arose in circles around Philip Neri. And he simply wanted to say – in contrast to the Protestants, who were then saying the papacy is at an end – through an endlessly long series of popes yet to come: 'No, it is not at an end.' But you don't have to conclude that it really ceases then. His series was never going to be long enough.

What did you like least of all about your office?

The many political visits, I would say. It was always pleasing, though, to speak concretely with heads of state and ambassadors, because you'd have lovely experiences. They are mostly people of spiritual interest, even if they are not Christians. But for me the political element was somehow the most laborious.

Was there something about which you felt discontented with yourself?

Yes, sure; for example that I did not always have the energy to express the catechesis as penetratingly and as humanly as possible.

Let's say this: your rhetoric was very reserved, you made little eye contact during lectures and your voice sounded rather monotonous. Was that intentional?

No, no. I was modest, and I have to admit also, often not powerful enough with my voice, and I frequently had not yet inwardly absorbed the text enough to be able to present it more freely. It was certainly a weakness, and my voice is weak in itself.

Indeed. Your strength, though, is being able to speak mostly in a way that is almost polished enough for your words to be published in book form immediately.

But when one has to speak as much and as often as a Pope must, one tends to be overexerted.

The Pope has a lot of people around him, and meets important people constantly. But are there not also lonely hours, in which one can feel terribly alone inside?

Certainly, but because I feel so connected to the Lord, I'm therefore never entirely alone.

He who believes is never alone?

Yes, genuinely. One simply knows, I'm not the one doing things. I also could not do it alone, He is constantly there. I must only listen, and make myself wide open for Him. And also share things with the closest collaborators.

How do you do this listening and opening wide for him? If you could give me some advice here . . .

[Laughs]

How does one do it best?

Well, now, you just beg the Lord – You must help me now! – and recollect yourself inwardly, stay silent. Then one can time and again knock on the door with prayer, and thus, you're already doing it.

What would you like to have occupied yourself more with in life?

Of course I would like to have worked intellectually more. 'Revelation', 'Scripture', 'Tradition', and 'What is theology as an academic discipline?', this was the field of topics that I wanted to elaborate better intellectually: something I could not do. But I'm nevertheless content with the other turn of events, with what has happened. The loving God wanted something different. That is obviously then the right thing for me now.

After so many decades, doesn't one lose even a bit of faith in one's own guild, in the power of theology and theologians?

German university theology is certainly in a crisis and needs new minds, new energy, a new intensity of faith. But theology itself is always on the move in new ways. I am grateful to the loving God that I could do what I did, even if I see it in its more modest dimensions, as the fruit of particular occasions, as pastoral–spiritual work. What I could do, as I said, is something other than what I wanted – I wanted my whole life long to be a real professor – but afterwards I see it was good how it went.

With you having been a professor, the title endured in a way. They named you 'Professor Pope' and 'Theology Pope'. Do you feel they got you right?

I would say I tried above all to be a shepherd. The passionate dealings with the Word of God are also included, of course, so I did things which a professor does. Added to that, I tried to be a confessor. The concepts *professor* and *confessor* philologically mean much the same thing, whereby the task lies more in the direction of confessor.

What do you look on as your weak side?

Maybe clear, purposeful governance and the decisions that have to be made there. I am just in that aspect actually more a professor, someone who deliberates and reflects on intellectual matters. So practical governance is not my forte, and there, I would say, is a certain weakness.

And what do you think you did a particularly good job of?

[Laughs] That I don't know.

In your autobiography there is often talk of 'new hardships'. Do you have the feeling that you've had a difficult life?

I would not say so. I mean, there are always difficulties and tribulations, but so many beautiful things too, that I would not say it was a difficult life, no.

What can still be learned in old age, and particularly as Pope?

Well, one can always learn. First, one must continue learning what the faith says to us in this time. And one must learn humility more, simplicity, readiness to suffer, and courage for resistance. On the other hand, one must learn to go further in openness and willingness.

As Pope were you a reformer, a preserver, or as your critics say, a failure?

I cannot see myself as a failure. I did my eight years in service. There were many difficulties in my time, if one thinks of the paedophile scandal, the stupid Williamson case, or even just Vatileaks. But on the whole it was indeed also a time in which many people newly found the faith and a great positive movement was there.

Reformer or preserver?

One must always do both. You have to renew things, and in that regard I tried to lead the faith forward, working from a modern concern. At the same time continuity is needed, to ensure that the faith is not torn down, or torn to pieces.

Were you happy then, being Pope?

[Laughs] Well, I would say so; I knew that I am carried, so I am grateful for many beautiful experiences. But it was always a burden too, of course.

In order to come to your current situation as Papa emeritus, which is something that has never before happened in Church history: could one say that Joseph Ratzinger, Pope Benedict, the man of reason, the bold thinker, ends up as a monk, as a person at prayer, where reason alone is not enough?

Yes, that is right.

The question which concerns us anew time and time again is: where is this God, actually, of whom we speak, from whom we hope for help? How and where can one locate Him? We now see further out into the universe, with the millions of planets, the countless solar systems, but as far as we can see now, nowhere is there anything that can be thought of as remotely like heaven, where God is supposedly enthroned.

[Laughs]. Yes, because there is not something, a place, where He sits. God Himself is the place beyond all places. If you look into the world, you do not see heaven, but you see traces of God everywhere. In the structure of matter, in all the rationality of reality. Even where you see human beings, you find traces of God. You see vices, but you also see goodness, love. These are the places where God is there.

You must completely do away with these old spatial notions, as they really do not work any more. Because the all is certainly not infinite in the strict sense of the word, although it is so vast that we humans may refer to it as infinite. And God cannot be found in some place inside or outside; rather, His presence is something wholly other.

It is very important that we renew our thinking in many respects, completely clear away these spatial things, and grasp matters afresh. So, just as there is an emotional presence between human beings – two human beings can touch each other emotionally across continents, because the human soul is a dimension which is different to the spatial dimension – so God is not in some place, but rather He is the reality which upholds all reality. And for this reality I don't need any kind of 'where', because 'where' is already a limitation, already no longer the infinite, the creator, who is the all, who sweeps over all time and is not Himself time, for He creates time and is always present.

I believe we have to change a lot here, just as our whole image of humanity has also changed. We don't have a six-thousand-year history any longer [as stated in the biblical chronology as an image], but a history I don't know how many more years old. Let us be open to these hypothetical numbers now. In any case, with this knowledge the structure of time in history is depicted differently today. Here theology still has to go thoroughly to work and provide human beings with conceptual possibilities again. Here the translation of theology and faith into the language of today has tremendous lacunae. Here there is much to do; to bring forth new conceptual schemes, and to help human beings to understand today that they are not to look for God in any kind of place.

Is God then somehow a spirit, an energy? Christian faith, however, speaks of a personal God.

Quite. Precisely His being *person* means that He is not in some place which is circumscribable. And to us human beings the person is that which transcends mere space and opens up the infinite to me. I can be here and somewhere else at the same time. I am not only there, just where my body is, but rather I live in an expanse. Precisely because He is person I cannot fix Him to a physical location, because 'person' is something encompassing, person is the other, person is greater.

Do you have any representation of God?

No.

As in Judaism?

Yes, OK, in as much, of course, that God is there in Jesus Christ, there in a human being.

'Anyone who has seen me has seen the Father'?[1]

Yes. Then He is genuinely depictable here.

You are now, as you expressed it, in the last phase of life. Can one prepare oneself for death?

I think one must, even. Not in the sense of performing particular actions, but living inwardly, so that there is a final self-examination before God. So that one goes out of this world and will be there before God, and before the saints, and before friends and those who weren't friends. So that one, let's say, accepts the finitude of this life and approaches it inwardly, to come before God's countenance.

How do you do that?

Just in my meditation. I time and time again think on the fact that it is going to end. I try to open myself up for it, and above all, to keep myself present. The important thing is not actually that I imagine it, but that I live in the consciousness of it, that all of life ascends to an encounter.

What should be on your gravestone?

[Chuckles] I would say: nothing! Only the name.

Your bishop motto comes to mind: 'Co-worker of the truth'.[2] *How did you actually come to that?*

---

[1] John 14.9.
[2] From 3 John 8.

Like this: I had for a long time excluded the question of truth, because it seemed to be too great. The claim: 'We have the truth!' is something which no one had the courage to say, so even in theology we had largely eliminated the concept of truth. In these years of struggle, the 1970s, it became clear to me: if we omit the truth, what do we do anything for? So truth must be involved.

Indeed, we cannot say 'I have the truth', but the truth has us, it touches us. And we try to let ourselves be guided by this touch. Then this phrase from John 3 crossed my mind, that we are 'co-workers of the truth'. One can work with the truth, because the truth is person. One can let truth in, try to provide the truth with value. That seemed to me finally to be the very definition of the profession of a theologian; that he, when he has been touched by this truth, when truth has caught sight of him, is now ready to let it take him into service, to work on it and for it.

'Co-worker of the truth' would actually be something for your gravestone.

Certainly, yes. I would say if it's already my motto you can set it on my gravestone.

A last question for this last testament. Love is one of your central themes, as a student, as a professor, as Pope. Where was love in your life? Where have you felt love, tasted love, experienced love with profound feelings? Or was it more of a theoretical, philosophical matter?

No. No, no. If one has not felt it, then one cannot talk of it. I felt it first at home with my father, my mother, my siblings. And, well, I wouldn't like to go into private details now, but I have been touched by it in different dimensions and forms. To be loved and to love another are things I have increasingly recognized as fundamental, so that one can live; so that one can say yes to oneself, so that one can say yes to another. Finally, it has become increasingly clear to me that God is not, let's say, a ruling power, a distant force; rather he is love and he loves me – and as such, life should be guided by him, by this power called love.

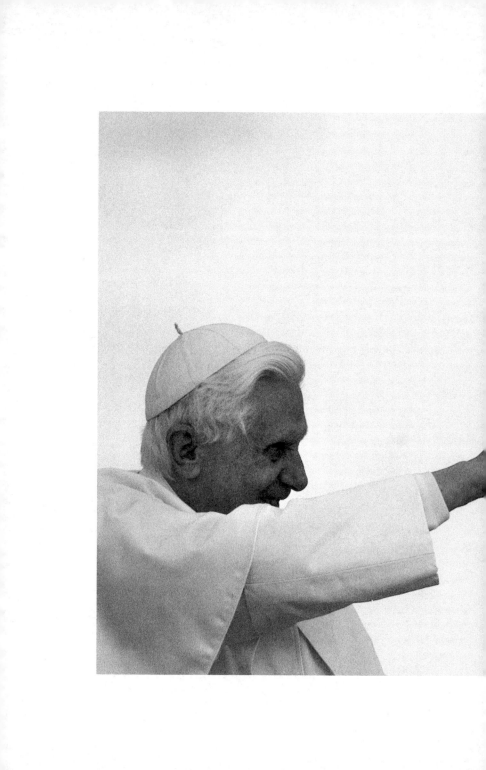

Author's Notes – compiled by Peter Seewald

Chapter 1

i *Nunc dimittis* are the first words of the Canticle of Simeon. They come from the biblical account of the Presentation of the Lord in the Temple of Jerusalem (Lk. 2.29–32). The aged Simeon recognizes Jesus Christ as the expected Messiah, praises God and now feels ready to die: 'At last all-powerful Father / you give leave to your servant / to go in peace according to your promise. / For my eyes have seen your salvation / which you have prepared for all people. / A light to enlighten the Gentiles / and give glory to your people Israel.'

ii The 'General Prayer' of St Peter Canisius, the 'Second Apostle of Germany': 'Almighty and eternal God, Lord, Heavenly Father! Look through the eyes of your gratuitous mercy at our sorrow, misery, and need. Have mercy on all the faithful Christians, for whom your only-begotten Son, our beloved Lord and saviour, Jesus Christ, willingly went into the hands of sinners and shed his precious blood on the trunk of the cross. Through this Lord Jesus avert, gracious Father, the well-deserved punishment, present and future threats, shameful rebellions, war, famine, disease, sad, and miserable times. Also enlighten and strengthen all worldly and spiritual rulers and leaders in all goods, so they convey what is to your divine honour, to our salvation, to general peace, and the welfare of all Christianity. Grant us, O God of peace, a right union in faith, without any division and separation; without any separation and schism, convert our hearts to true repentance and amendment of our lives; kindle in us the fire of your love, give us a hunger and a zeal for all righteousness, so that we are as pleasing and complacent to you as obedient children in life and in death. We pray also, as you want, O God, that we should pray, for our friends and enemies, the healthy and the sick, for all sad and sorrowful Christians, for all the living and the dead, to you O Lord, is commended all our deeds, our trade and commerce, our living and dying. Let us enjoy thy grace here and get there with all the elect that we might praise you in eternal joy and blessedness, honour and praise. We want to give praise, honour and glory to you! Grant us that, O Lord, heavenly Father, through Jesus Christ your beloved Son, who lives with you and the Holy Spirit as the same God and rules from eternity to eternity, Amen!'

Chapter 3

i In the interview with the Jesuit magazine *Civiltà Cattolica*, published in September 2013, Pope Francis answered questions about his life-story, his thinking and his understanding of the Church.

Chapter 4

i After Marktl, Tittmoning and Aschau, the family moved in April 1937 to a small old farmhouse in the village of Hufschlag in Traunstein, which the father had purchased in 1933 for 5,500 Reichsmark. Immediately after Hitler came to power, he was convinced: 'Now comes the war, now we need a house.'

Chapter 7

i The French mathematician and philosopher Blaise Pascal had a mystical experience in 1654, which he recorded in his famous *Memorial* (reminder sheet), a text on a narrow strip of parchment, which he always carried with him. God is not to be found by thinking, it says, not in philosophical proofs of God ('not the God of philosophers and scholars'), but he had an experience like fire, where he expressly alludes to the story of the burning bush and refers to the 'God of Abraham, God of Isaac, God of Jacob': Exod. 3.6.

Chapter 12

i Excerpt from the 'Regensburg speech' of 12 September 2006, in which Benedict XVI quoted the Byzantine Emperor Manuel II Palaiologos: 'Without descending to details, such as the difference in treatment accorded to those who have the "Book" and the "infidels", he addresses his interlocutor with a startling brusqueness, a brusqueness that we find unacceptable, on the central question about the relationship between religion and violence in general, saying: "Show me just what Mohammed brought that was new, and there you will find things only evil and inhuman, such as his command to spread by the sword the faith he preached." The emperor, after having expressed himself so forcefully, goes on to explain in detail the reasons why spreading the faith through violence is something unreasonable. Violence is incompatible with the nature of God and the nature of the soul...'

ii There is an intense debate about the Good Friday prayer for the Jews, one of the 'General Intercessions' in the Good Friday liturgy of the Roman rite. The original version dates back to the sixth century. It called the Jews *perfidi* ('faithless'), and asked God to take the 'veil from their hearts', to give them the knowledge of Christ and to rescue them from 'blindness' and 'darkness'. In the course of action taken during the liturgical reform of the Second Vatican Council, Paul VI changed the wording. Today, the following text is spoken on Good Friday at the usual service: 'Let us pray for the Jewish people, the first to hear the word of God, that they may continue to grow in the love of his name and in faithfulness to his covenant. Almighty and eternal God, long ago you gave your promise to Abraham and his posterity. Hear your Church as we pray that the people you first made your own may arrive at the fullness of redemption.' When John Paul II permitted bishops to allow the old rite to the Missal of 1962 for certain groups, the different version of the Jewish prayer was again possible, including the statements that the Jews were in a 'delusion' and would have 'their darkness wrested'. Benedict XVI changed this version in February 2008 to the wording: 'Let us also pray for the Jews: That our God and Lord may illuminate their hearts, that they acknowledge Jesus Christ is the Saviour of all men. Almighty and eternal God, who want that all men be saved and come to the recognition of the truth, propitiously grant that even as the fullness of the peoples enters Thy Church, all Israel be saved. Through Christ Our Lord. Amen.' Only now – in 2016 – have I learned that one apparently has set headings on the individual petitions in the Old Missal, which do not belong to the old Missal and should therefore be eliminated. The heading on the intercession for the Jews is there, apparently, '*Pro conversione Iudaeorum*'. It does not belong to the text of the Old Missal. If you believe a heading is a heading, you should read 'Pro Iudaeis'.

Chapter 14

i   In January 2009, Benedict XVI announced a decree remitting the excommunication of four bishops of the Society of St Pius X, a fraternity of priests who had separated from the Church authorities in Rome, and this decree sparked an unparalleled media campaign against him.

To recall the chronology of the events:

The original reason for the excommunication was that the founder of the SSPX fraternity, Archbishop Marcel Lefebvre, had consecrated four bishops in 1988, against the wishes of the then Pope, John Paul II. Because this was a direct challenge to the authoritative primacy of the Pope, the bishops involved were excommunicated.

The grounds for this excommunication, however, were gone after the Fraternity acknowledged the Pope's primacy in a written statement. The bishops who had been consecrated could thus have their excommunications lifted. As a technical matter involving the canonical status of four individuals, this was not rehabilitation of the Fraternity's standing, or some kind of wholesale admission of SSPX into the bosom of the Church.

The Vatican had planned to announce the news that the Holy Father had remitted the excommunication of the four bishops at 12 p.m. on 24 January. But, a week earlier on 17 January, this news had already been anticipated by a Spanish journalist. On 20 January, *Der Spiegel* reported an interview on Swedish television in which one of the bishops whose excommunication was lifted – the Englishman Richard Williamson – had denied the Holocaust. On 22 January this interview was broadcast on Swedish television. On the same day the Vatican expert Andrea Tornielli brought the news of the Williamson interview to the daily newspaper *Il Giornale*. The Vatican likewise held a summit meeting on the issue. The participants in this meeting were: the

Cardinals from the Curia; Bertone, Hoyos, Levada, Hummes, and two bishops. The results of the meeting were inconclusive, nothing happened. At this time the Pope's private secretary, Georg Gänswein, was unwell in bed. The case became a political issue; all statements of the Vatican maintained defiantly that Holocaust deniers had nothing whatsoever to do with the Catholic Church. Benedict XVI, who only a few weeks previously had called for 'deep solidarity with the Jewish world', and emphasized the need to stand against any form of anti-Semitism, was now accused of anti-Semitism himself.

Timeline

1927

Born Joseph Alois Ratzinger on Holy Saturday, 16 April 1927, at 4.15 a.m. in Marktl am Inn, Altötting, baptized at 8.30 a.m. the same day.

His parents are the police chief Joseph Ratzinger (6 March 1877–25 August 1959) and the baker's daughter Maria Ratzinger (8 January 1884–16 December 1963).

He is the third child of the family, after Maria Theogena (7 December 1921–2 November 1991) and Georg (15 January 1924).

1929–42

11 July 1929
The family moves to Tittmoning.

5 December 1932
Moves to Aschau am Inn.

April 1937
Police chief Ratzinger retires; the family moves to Hufschlag, to a former farmhouse near Traunstein (built 1726).

1927
Admitted to the Gymnasium in Traunstein.

16 April 1939
Enters the diocesan seminary, St Michael's Seminary in Traunstein.

1943–5

August 1943–September 1944
Anti-aircraft assistant in Unterföhring, in Ludwigsfeld near Munich, and in Gilching am Ammersee.

Autumn 1944
Reich labour service in Burgenland, Austria.

13 December 1944
Conscripted into 'I. Schützen-Ausbildungskompanie des Grenadier-Ersatz- und Ausbildungs-Bataillons 179'.

May 1945
Deserts from the *Wehrmacht*.

May to 19 July 1945
Interned in an American POW camp near Neu-Ulm.

1946–59

3 January 1946–summer 1947
Studies philosophy at the Philosophisch-Theologische Hochschule in Freising, Bavaria. Then theology at the University of Munich.

Late autumn 1950–June 1951
Post-graduate work in Freising while preparing for priestly ordination.

29 June 1951
Ordained priest in Freising Cathedral.

From 1 July
Assistant priest in Munich-Moosach (St Martin).

From 1 August
Curate in Munich-Bogenhausen.

1 October 1952–1954
Lecturer at the Freising seminary.

1953
Doctorate in theology at University of Munich (Thesis: 'The People and the House of God in St Augustine's Doctrine of the Church').

From winter semester 1953/4
Representative of the professorial chair in dogmatic and fundamental theology at the College for Philosophy and Theology in Freising. Habilitation at the University of Munich in the discipline of fundamental theology (Thesis: 'The Theology of History in St Bonaventure'). A first attempt at the habilitation failed due to the resistance of Michael Schmaus.

1 January 1958
Appointed extraordinary professor for dogmatic and fundamental theology in Freising.

1959–63

Ordinary professor for fundamental theology at the University of Bonn. In August 1959 his father dies in Traunstein.

1962–5

Adviser to Cardinal Joseph Frings of Cologne and official conciliar theologian (*peritus*) at Vatican II. Member of the Doctrinal Committee of the German Bishops and of the International Pontifical Theological Commission in Rome.

1963–6

Ordinary professor for dogmatics and the history of dogma at the University of Münster. His mother dies in December 1963.

1966–9

Ordinary professor for dogmatics and the history of dogma at the University of Tübingen. In 1968 his work *Introduction to Christianity* published.

1969–77

Ordinary professor for dogmatics and the history of dogma and vice-rector of the University of Regensburg.

1977–81

25 March 1977
Appointed Archbishop of Munich and Freising by Pope Paul VI.

28 May 1977
Consecrated Bishop in Munich.

27 June 1977
Appointed Cardinal by Pope Paul VI.

25 November 1981
Appointed by John Paul II as Prefect of the Congregation for the Doctrine of the Faith, president of the Pontifical Biblical Commission and the International Theological Commission.

1982–2005

28 February 1982
Departure from Munich and Freising.

1986–92
Head of the Pontifical Commission for the Preparation of the *Catechism of the Catholic Church.*

2 November 1991
Death of his sister Maria, who has served him for thirty-four years as office assistant and housekeeper.

1992
Suffers a stroke and is hospitalized for several weeks.

7 November 1992
Elected member of the Académie des Sciences Morales et Politiques de l'Institut de France.

5 April 1993
Promoted to Cardinal Archbishop of the suburbicarian Diocese of Velletri-Segni.

1994
Member of the Congregation for Canonizations.

1998
Vice-dean of the College of Cardinals.

27 November 2002
Elected dean of the College of Cardinals.

2 April 2005
Death of John Paul II.

8 *April 2005*
As dean of the College of Cardinals Ratzinger presides at the funeral ceremonies for John Paul II.

2005–6

19 April 2005
Election of Joseph Ratzinger after the twenty-six-hour conclave in the fourth round of votes to became 265th Pope of the Catholic Church. Chooses name Benedict XVI and is the first German Pope since Adrian VI, for 482 years. Also the first Pope of the modern era to design his coat of arms without the tiara, a sign of secular power, replacing it with a simple bishop's mitre.

18 August 2005
Visit to World Youth Day in Cologne with a million participants.

2–23 October 2005
Presides over Synod of Bishops in Rome.

2006

Publication of the encyclical *Deus caritas est* (*God is Love*). Abolition of the title 'Patriarch of the West'. Beginning of a reform of the Curia with the merging of several papal councils. Pilgrimage to Poland with a visit to the Auschwitz concentration camp. Journey to the World Meeting of Families in Spain. Home visit to Bavaria. Istanbul meeting with Bartholomew I, the leading representative of the Orthodox Church.

2006–13

In the 2,872 days of his pontificate, Benedict XVI wrote 17 *Motu proprio* enactments, 116 Apostolic Constitutions and 144 Apostolic Exhortations. In addition, 278 public letters and 242 messages to church leaders and governments. Among his works are the encyclicals *Deus caritas est*, *Spe salvi* and *Caritas in veritate*. His fourth encyclical *Lumen fidei* was published by his successor. The Pope's Jesus trilogy sold millions of copies in twenty languages and reached believers in seventy-two different countries.

Benedict XVI conducted 352 liturgical celebrations, held 340 audiences (not including foreign travel and private audiences), and pronounced 62 people blessed and 28 saints. In addition to 27 special public prayers and 3,520 sermons, the Holy Father prayed the *Angelus/ Regina Coeli* 452 times with his faithful. In his tenure, he made a total of 1,491 addresses. He made 24 trips outside Italy (to 22 countries) and 30 trips within Italy. His appearances in Rome and Castel Gandolfo were attended by 18 million people.

11 February 2013
As the first Pope for a thousand years to resign, Benedict XVI, in the eighth year of his pontificate, announced his departure, which would take effect on 28 February 2013.

A Note on the Type

The text of this book is set in Bembo, which was first used in 1495 by the Venetian printer Aldus Manutius for Cardinal Bembo's *De Aetna*. The original types were cut for Manutius by Francesco Griffo. Bembo was one of the types used by Claude Garamond (1480–1561) as a model for his Romain de l'Université, and so it was a forerunner of what became the standard European type for the following two centuries. Its modern form follows the original types and was designed for Monotype in 1929.